CARRYING THE BRANCH
POETS IN SEARCH OF PEACE

Front cover art: © Tracy McQueen
Back cover art: *Aleppo Is My Breath Prayer,* 2017
Design & layout: Steven Asmussen
Copyediting: Linda E. Kim

Glass Lyre Press, LLC
P.O. Box 2693
Glenview, IL 60025
www.GlassLyrePress.com

CARRYING THE BRANCH

POETS IN SEARCH OF PEACE

Edited by
Diane Frank
Lois P. Jones
Ami Kaye
Rustin Larson
Gloria Mindock
Melissa Studdard

GLASS LYRE PRESS

In memory of Susan Elbe & James Reiss

Artists' Statements

"Carrying the Branch" by Tracy McQueen

Using mostly shades of grey and white for my color palette, I created a dark, foreboding sky from which the dove emerges, carrying an olive branch, bringing the hope of peace. Light emerging from darkness was the theme of this piece as my focus was to illustrate the idea that despite the atrocities committed by humanity, we can always find compassion for one another and extend a hand, or branch, in peace.

Digital Media: Photoshop CS6

"Aleppo is my Breath Prayer" mosaic, by Jason Brown, Emily Bynum, Jamie Daniel, Ainsley Fleetwood, Ruth Goring, Emily Klein, Katherine Lamb, Rebecca Larsen, and Olga Mest. Mounting by Ronald Frantz.

We think of this work as a lament for the ruin of the historic eastern sector of Aleppo during Syria's intense, protracted civil war, but also as a way to honor the many brave people who helped each other in the midst of it all—doctors who worked underground; the White Helmets who dug people out of the rubble after bombings; neighbors who kept each other's spirits up. We especially wanted to recognize the work of the Syrian American Medical Society. So we have small bright objects embedded among the gray and dark-colored tiles.

In the Christian mystical tradition, a breath prayer is a word or phrase that you repeat quietly in the ordinary rhythm of inhalation and exhalation. Our work is an expression of our prayers for peace, justice, and restoration in the beautiful country of Syria.

Contents

II — Diane Frank

III — Lois P. Jones

IV — Rustin Larson

VI — Melissa Studdard

AMI KAYE

The idea for this book came about immediately following the Paris 2015 attack. Our reactions ranged from disbelief, anger, helplessness to despair. The past few years have been rife with terror attacks, wars, civil unrest, oppression, political strife and numerous other crises that have caused unbelievable devastation all around the world. Although it is impossible to address every problem, we no longer have the option to turn away. The knowledge that our contribution may only be a drop in the bucket cannot keep us from trying. For all the hate, violence, and ugliness present in the world, there is also great selflessness, sacrifice and beauty.

In this book readers will find an eclectic mix of styles, treatments, and topics that resound with purpose. Each editor has painstakingly culled pieces in the hope that the diverse and powerful voices create synergy for this cause. The first section reflects some of the submissions sent to Glass Lyre Press for this project, while other pieces were solicited.

We are deeply grateful to all the immensely talented poets who contributed their work for this project; editors Diane Frank, Lois P. Jones, Rustin Larson, Gloria Mindock, and Melissa Studdard for commendable care in curating their sections while keeping true to the vision of this anthology; artist Tracy McQueen for her evocative dove carrying an olive branch and Ruth Goring and team for creating the Aleppo mosaic on the back cover. Thanks also to volunteers who have pitched in to help and, most of all, our readers who purchased this book and in doing so continue to spread a positive message and directly help people impacted by terrorism and unrest.

Our work does not end with the release of this book; there is so much more to do. We all want a better, stronger, more peaceful world, but how do we begin to fight xenophobia, racism, hate, terrorism, political strife, and war? In this disturbing, chaotic time the words of Martin Luther King, Jr. provide direction yet again: "Darkness cannot drive out darkness; only light can do that. Hate cannot drive out hate; only love can do that."

Think of how much love we could spread in the world. Let us do this together—it is the only way we have a chance.

John Amen

American Myths #14
for Philip

I'm the black son; doesn't matter if this is factual,
it's my life story, the metaphor that locks my throat.
Raised in a flooded town, I belly-crawled dirt roads
in a county of Stars & Bars, pale Jesus & pit bulls,
succubi lying open-legged in a hayloft. My eleventh
birthday, I grabbed the rattler from the priest, held

its face to my face. I watched its eyes turn to glass
as the congregation booed. Don't believe the white
father, his myth of origin; truth is, he turns a crank
in the background, he keeps the keys, he sprays the
fig tree with pesticide when believers aren't looking.
Don't entertain that crap about the dead mother being

sculpted from a rib, bear in mind that this white father
is simply another white father in a line of white fathers,
each of whom burned in a pyre of Jacksons, screwed
by his own ballyhoo. That said, there are indeed doors
in the white father's house that can only be opened
by a black son. Not every black son. This black son.

Patricia Clark

West of Syria

They washed up on a beach, the small
                    bodies of children—
    a little boy of just three years.
                    It was not the sea's fault.

It was not the fault of the rubber raft.
                    We do not have life jackets so small,
        the smugglers said. It will be brief,
                            the crossing to Italy, they added.

The gendarme takes a photo, then picks up
                    the boy's body—wearing shorts, a bright
                            summer top, and sandals. Once,
    there was a future, smiles, laughter,
                    once he had a brother and mother.

They drowned in the same sea. It was not
                    a blessing that the father lived.
        The mother was twenty-seven years old.
                    What they wanted was a better life.
    To want is to risk, and to take a chance
                    is how a risk is made tangible.

            Into the smugglers' hands, crumpled bills.
    When the rubber raft came,
                    the father objected. Will we be safe?

The boy washed up on a beach, the waves
                    lapping against his still mouth,
                            as though he were sleeping,
    as though you could make a pillow of sand.

Lori Desrosiers

Praise to the Earth

Praise to the ocean, waves and foam, bright reef fish hiding in anemone, sharks and whales doze below, above them cormorants and gannets float. To waves that roll into shore at night, the moon reflecting sea foam's white, the breakers in sync with our breathing as the buoy bell sings in the harbor.

Praise to tiny creatures, amoebae and molds, bacteria, to the algae sisters Chloro, Phaeo and Rhodophyta, green and blue-green. lichen, moss and plankton. Praise to nanobes and eukaryotes.

Praise to beach roses, pink under street lights; to peonies, iris and lilac; even at midnight inhale the scent; to the bees, safe in their hive, to evening clouds, white moon behind them; summer rain, watering the gardens.

Praise to writers and scribblers, fruit in the bowl, mat on the table, water in the mug. To the record on the turntable, the hat on the hat stand, the coat on the chair.

Praise to new parents walking a baby, to the restless soldier home from war. Praise to the peacemakers.

To poets, listeners to the night noises, cicadas, clapping of wings. To snorers and dreamers, singers in their sleep. Praise to the Earth, our home.

Diane Frank

A View from the Moon

As we move into the darker time,
my friends are scattered around a globe
rocked by hurricanes and tsunamis.
Where does the soul find leaves
for its unexpressed longing
in a forest of bare trees?

I would like to believe that love
finds its way in the world.
My voice is breaking
as I push myself through the keyhole
to the shimmer of light
on the other side.

At the edge of the continent,
I find a necklace of broken pottery,
a spiral of conch,
a lacework of pelican prints
in the sand.

I search for Buddha
in a Chinatown market,
the single note that vibrates,
the moment of the vulnerable heart
where I wake up inside an Appalachian fiddle tune
in the minor key of the mountains.

There's a footprint in the sand of the soul,
before people deviate
from the path their soul has chosen.
In the crashing waves after midnight,
where does the soul
find the imprint of its longing?

In the sand I piece together
fragments of broken clay
with a desire to transmute
everything that is not holy
in a world that is still finding its form.

What we can't express
becomes the planetary nightmare.
The soul hydroplanes, slips off the road.
In the early morning moonlight,
a black spider
crawling over my leg
with its message.

But I wake up from the dream of a man
who hypnotized me
spinning
in a hot tub
and made my cello float.

I am the woman on the moon,
a crescent of possibilities
at the edge of the constellation
where night becomes morning,
Isis holding the ankh on her throne
in a robe that matches the midnight sky.
She tells me I need to start expecting
the good things to come true.

On the Earth, a depression and a hysteria –
a memory of Minoan times,
an oracle in the rock
Arctic Wilderness
River Gorge,
a clay vessel filling with light
as my vision becomes the music
becomes the man,
and climbs into bed with me.
I want in all ways
to be a blessing.

Ruth Goring

August 4, 2011
Hama, Syria

It was the day of shouts and ragged marching
and the clipped answering shots of rifles,
tanks squatting in our central square
with heavy self-assurance.
The day women darted and fell
in terrible piles with their children.
The call to prayer came to our ears
with throbbing dust, and then silence
descended to spread its ancient carpet.
It was the day our hearts lay on the sidewalk
like batteries leaking acid, stilled
in the heat of that unending day
that kept peering through smoke-curtains
and deciding to wait, to keep waiting.

Ruth Goring

The thirty doctors of eastern Aleppo

1. The snipers' game
Each day it is different.
Those felled while crossing
the Corridor of Death
are brought in to us.

One day it is small boys,
black curls tousled, eyes imploring
or mortally still.
Sometimes it is a body part:
the right shoulder or
the neck.

Then they choose pregnant women.
One is carried in, abaya bunched and
sticky with blood.
The bullet has pierced her belly,
found its nest in the fetal brain.

2. Floors
The regime bombs hospitals.
We work underground.

Sometimes the stairs are slick.
Sometimes everything is crimson.

Haste, haste. An IV
for this grandfather on the floor.
Swabbing for this twelve-year-old,
the wound below her collarbone
red like an astonished
second mouth.

3. Evacuation
We bear them onto buses,
pack them snugly
between the healthy, cradle
their heads with rolled sheets.

We inch toward Idlib,
inshallah. On Aleppo's torn fringe
the bus stops for hours,
something about shooting—
soldiers mill about
in high spirits, a gray man
wanders with a sheaf of papers.

The bus wheezes, moves again at last.
I am holding the hand of a child,
her head wrapped in bandages,
her hands minute,
the lightest petals.
As we turn off the M5, leave the preserve,
they rise like whispers,
her lungs heave
in the tight cylinder of her chest,
then fall, all the green leaves of her
and all her branches.

Hedy Habra

The Green Line
Lebanon (1975-1990)

was drawn in front of my father-in-law's
      four-story building
on Rue de Damas
      Tarik El Sham   the road to Damascus

We lived on the fourth floor
      were the first to leave
then the family on the second floor left

then the Melkite Orthodox Divorce Settlement
      Centre bronze plaque
was taken down
      from the first floor's door

Fighters placed heavy artillery on the terrace
      shooting aimlessly
across the Green Line

From the balcony my sister-in-law saw
a silhouette
      crossing Rue de Damas
from the St Joseph University

a red pool spread over the black asphalt
      (of the infamous Green Line)
snipers
      snipers
everywhere
      My father-in-law took his family and left

In Tucson, he raised canaries
      grew curly cucumber   *mouloukhiyeh*
vines for stuffing mint & thyme

An old man with a weak heart
                  he returned three times
to rebuild what was left

he kept returning with his music
and water pipe,
                recalling the days when
he'd just cross Rue de Damas

      to play backgammon
at the café terraces

Hedy Habra

Salawat
Lament of an old Lebanese.

I have lost count
of nights
lulling myself to sleep,
magical signs,
salawat, unheard
pleas,
my rosary,
restrung so many times,
I can no longer
distinguish
Ave from Gloria.
I could be imploring Allah,
my beads
the same size
as my neighbor Yasmine's
who lost
two sons.

All of us
people
of the Book,
all faithful, burned incense,
knelt
in the right direction,
all wept
at the wakes of loved ones.
Now, in each home
an oil lamp lights
black picture frames.
A flat stone
pressed
against my heart,

the used-up
words, eroding
the tip of our tongue,
our lips, our soul,
keep coming,
salawat,
soothing
like water falling
over
boulders.

*Salawat means prayers in Arabic

Jane Hirshfield

Anywhere You Look

in the corner of a high rain gutter
under the roof tiles
new grasses' delicate seed heads
what war, they say

Jane Hirshfield

Three Mornings

In Istanbul, my ears
three mornings heard the early call to prayer.
At fuller light, heard birds then,
waterbirds and treebirds, birds of migration.
Like three knowledges,
I heard them: incomprehension,
sweetened distance, longing.
When the body dies, where will they go,
those migrant birds and prayer calls,
as heat from sheets when taken from a dryer?
With voices of the ones I loved,
great loves and small loves, train wheels,
crickets, clock-ticks, thunder—where will they,
when in fragrant, tumbled heat they also leave?

Rustin Larson

Before Work

6:35 a.m. Not suffering. The quietest time
Of morning. I can hear a train rumbling
Miles away. A "Charles Pretzels" can serves
As a waste basket. The rodent digs
Litter under its spinning wheel. My senses say
Attack another expectation. Run by another
Temporary solution. I think I'll make oatmeal.
I haven't heard a thing happen yet.

The magnifying glass sleeps with the geode.
Maybe I want to run. It's starting to lighten.
Birds by the millions, flying away. Vienna
Waltzes. Imagine never to hear Strauss again.
You are up and dressed and smiling. I gulp
Down my requirement of water. Prepare.
It's amazing how easily things don't rhyme.
Iggy Pop. Waltzes. The Spectrum.

Well anyway, it's off to work. My legs are
Sending me a message. The begonias, white and red,
Guard my doorstep. The girls are still asleep.
That train is finally blowing through town, past
The wrecked iron works, past New Chicago
And the falafel place. It's 6:50. I think
It's safe to go outside. In the quiet rain.
Past the people who haven't any plans.

Lyn Lifshin

Later As The Gardener Gently
Touched a Few Green Leaves

growing out of
the top of an
otherwise barren
stick of a tree.
"This one was hit
by shrapnel but
it is alive. The tree
will live and we
will live." The
essence of
the world is
a flower

Lyn Lifshin

Syrian Boy

cries for Dad
after losing
both legs in
a blast. "Pick
me up Daddy,"
he cries "pick
me up, pick
me up"

Giuseppe Nibali

Letter of Samir to His First Love

Translated by Helen Wickes & Pina Piccolo

My beloved
I beg you not to die
While I arrive and rain on Libya
Please, don't die. You who had breasts
the same as other breasts and eyes and skin
the color of dark wood.

Tomorrow, Italy, that slice from the sea
for me, one who is good in the desert, in the races
on sand.
May Allah quicken this distance as short
As a shell thrown to the other side,
and keep yourself alive there,
because the sun depends on your glance.
If I live you will be my future. If I live
you will have these letters and I'll hear again
the sound of your eyelids opening.

Tomorrow Italy, that slice in the belly,
that violin crying.

Giuseppe Nibali

Lettera di Samir alla sua prima bellezza

Mio adorato amore,
ti prego non morire.
Mentre arrivo e piovo sulla Libia,
non morire. Tu hai avuto seni
uguali ad altri seni e occhi e pelle
di legno scuro.

Domani l'Italia, questo taglio nel mare
per me, buono al deserto, alle corse
di sabbia.
Che Allah faccia breve questo tiro
di conchiglia, ma tieniti viva lì,
che il sole dipende da uno sguardo.
Se vivrò tu sarai mio futuro. Se vivrò
avrai queste carte e faranno ancora
rumore le palpebre che apri.
Domani l'Italia, questo taglio nel ventre,
questo pianto di violino.

Giulio Gasperini

Salt

Translated by Helen Wickes, Pina Piccolo & Donald Stang

Salt that is heavy — that weighs down our garments — salt
that burns like sun rising from the water.
A gaze cast upon the foaming wave.
A distant land, a jutting rock,
the distant sound of songs from home. There
Lampedusa (perhaps I'm wrong) I don't know
its name — I don't understand the sextant — the
hand reaching out, which I can no longer grasp.
Here there's salt that burns, we breathe sweat,
salt that slakes a thirst of distant hours and hours,
lost in the salt of water that reminds you
of longing and which alone betrays deliverance.

Giulio Gasperini

Sale

Sale che grava – che pesa i vestiti – sale
che brucia come sole che sale dall'acqua.
Lo sguardo gettato sull'onda schiumante.
Una terra distante, uno scoglio sporgente,
il suono lontano di canzoni materne. Là
Lampedusa (magari mi sbaglio) il suo
nome ignoro – non conosco il sestante – la
mano che sporge, che non so più afferrare.
Qua c'è sale che brucia, si respira sudore,
un sale che placa una sete di ore e ore
remote, perse nel sale di un'acqua che sa
di vaghezza e che sola inganna salvezza.

Tareq Al Jabr

Attribute

Translated by Donald Stang & Pina Piccolo

While the slaughter of the people
And the trembling of the neighborhoods
exhaust themselves
at the din of all the firing
I contemplate a sparrow who knows not how to move,
still as a statue
without an inner spirit.

I conceal myself in a corner
looking out at the weapons of death
I cover my eyes, I will not see snipers shoot at my eyes.

Then the sparrow begins singing his melody,
the chirping he chooses
from within
is his only attribute
for proclaiming who he is.

Tareq Al Jabr

Attributo

Mentre si consuma
l'eccidio della gente
ed il fremito dei quartieri
al frastuono di spari
contemplo un passerotto che muoversi non sa
è una statua immobile
senza spirito dentro essa.

Mi nascondo in un angolo
affacciato sulle armi della morte
copro i miei occhi, non vedrò cecchini sparare ai miei occhi.

Poi inizia il passerotto a intonare la sua melodia,
da dentro
sceglie il cinguettio
suo unico attributo
per gridare chi è.

Pina Piccolo

Warning from the Shores
Translated by Donald Stang and Pina Piccolo

A message of fire
Contained in a lifeboat instead of a bottle
The shore does not recoil
The message explodes
On the threshhold of Europe
Before the stunned cliffs
of the Bay of Rabbits
With their unsuspecting expression
Jolted by the tremor of the Earth
Only the Earth detecting the warning.

Pina Piccolo

Avviso dalle sponde

Messaggio di fuoco
In bottiglia di barcone
Non si ritrae la sponda
Esplode
In limine d'Europa
Davanti al volto stupito dei Conigli
Dall'aria ignara
Scossi dal tremito della Terra
Unica sensibile all'avviso.

Connie Post

To A Woman Lost on the Road
in Afghanistan

I wish I could tell you
where your son is

I wish I could tell you
why the mosque
is fractured

or why the ruined moon
has dropped its shrapnel
in your lap

or why there
are not enough
prosthesis
for everyone
who is missing a limb

I can only stand here
and offer these beads
of contrition
that may
or may not
find the crater
of your open hands

Connie Post

"Witness Survives by Pretending to be Dead"

Another Mass Shooting in the News

I can only wonder
if a fallen soldier from Nam
reached out from long ago
and whispered in her ear
"this is how it's done"

she must have paused –
heard the legend
of stillness

a voice of gravel
must have set her
in a mud grey battlefield
helped her notice
the faded coats of enemies

in buckling of the knees
I wonder if her bones
invoked the knowledge
of the omega wolf

crouching
rolling on its back
into a submissive dusk

as she fell,
did she know that time
has stretch marks

or how − as years pass
survival becomes
a false shadow

she could not have known then
that years later
she will listen for the voices
of muddy soldiers
beg the jagged night
for air
for shards of mercy

every night
she will cut
a new opening to her mouth
and still
nobody will listen

Megan Merchant

Road Closure, Aleppo

When I hear, on the radio,
that your road is closed,

I think of the desert monsoon
that razed the edges
of our highway,

the only way out—
overcome

and how, completely stuck,

I thought it looked the way
my mother did when
she tucked her lower lip

to dam
the words
that wanted to leave

but would wash out
the bridge of every conversation
she had to try politely
to cross

simply because she
was a woman,

which meant she had
lips that would riven
and silt.

But closing our road
did not mean
that fruit and meat
would rot scarce,

or hold us inside a city crumbed,
where raids shamble night
and the sky is filagreed with smoke,
not stars,

and I do not have dreams
where bullets knock
door to door
looking under beds
for my children,

wanting to gnarl their
hair with sulfured breath.

I imagine you, other mother,
who know your children
cannot swim,

but that also they cannot sleep
when the walls
are broken piano keys
thudding

and hunger is a wing
flapping
against barbed ribs,

and each lullaby is sung
under a dry tongue
waltzing inside of your mouth.

When our road closed
the neighborhood kids

inflated rafts
to float the flood-mile
for fun

and it was lightning
that blackened the ground,
thunder that bucked against fences.

I imagine, if I could touch
your hand, we would both say
that destruction is a root of nature,

but whelmed
under our tongues—
the word that means *man*.

Aimee Nezhukumatathil

Mr. Cass and The Crustaceans

Whales the color of milk have washed ashore
in Germany, their stomachs clogged full
of plastic and car parts. Imagine the splendor
of a creature as big as half a football field—

the magnificence of the largest brain
of any animal—modern or extinct. I have
been trying to locate my fourth grade
science teacher for years. Mr. Cass, who

gave us each a crawfish he found just past
the suburbs of Phoenix, before strip malls
licked every good desert with a cold blast
of Freon and glass. Mr. Cass who played

soccer with us at recess, who let me check
on my wily, snappy crawfish in the plastic
blue pool before class started so I could place
my face to the surface of the water and see

if it still skittered alive. I hate to admit
how much this meant to me, the only brown girl
in the classroom. How I wish I could tell Mr. Cass
how I've never stopped checking the waters—

the ponds, the lakes, the sea. And I worry
that I've yet to see a sperm whale, except when
they beach themselves in coves. How many songs
must we hear from the sun-bleached bones

of a seabird or whale? If there were anyone on earth
who would know this, Mr. Cass, it's you—how even
bottle caps found inside a baby albatross corpse
can make a tiny ribcage whistle when the ocean wind

blows through it just right—I know wherever you are,
you'd weep if you heard this sad music. I think
how you first taught us kids how to listen to water,
and I'm grateful for each story in its song.

Kalpna Singh-Chitnis

Trespassing My Ancestral Lands

In my dreams,
I often trespass my ancestral lands,

looking for the centuries
hidden in the hills,

finding the history
lost in the sand,

searching for an oracle
safe in the ruins,

not to be found
and read.

I often venture,
without any food or water,

in the land of five rivers,
emerging through the passages of a glorious civilization.

I have no shoes, only my garb, and a scarf,
that I'm afraid of losing to the desert winds.

An amulet strung around my neck
reads an Aayat of the Quran;

May almighty bless the daughter of an idol worshiper,
out to defy the borders and demarcations,

there were only destinations,
before the birth of nations.

In my dreams,
I often wonder,

who carved my face
and disappeared in the winds?

I wonder,
where my ancestors came from?

Were they Aryan, Mughal or Turk?
Greek, Mongol or Tughluq?

What mountains did they cross?
What oceans did they brave?

And the roads they traveled,
were they made of silk, rocks or gravel?

What battles did they fight,
before surrendering to the light?

Where did they sleep, away from their homes?
In *Ordo*, Palaces or *Viharas*?

What food did they eat?
What songs did they write and sing?

Did they speak Sanskrit, Prakrit,
Farsi or Pashto?

I run bewildered in the desert,
like a dervish;

like a Sufi,
leaving behind a trail of songs,

for a caravan lost in
the desert storms...

In my dreams,

I search for the *Buddha* in the forest,
and *Muhammad* in a cave.

I look for *Krishna* in the battlefields,
and *Chanakya* in *Takshashila.*

In the alleys of towns and villages,
I look for *Ghalib, Rumi* and Khayyám,

In the temples, I look for *Meera, Kabir* and *Tulsi,*
and *Rama* in a *gurukul.*

In my dreams,
I remain uncaptured.

In my dreams,
my dreams are valid.

In my dreams,
I sleep in the seven continents,

and rise with the sun
on the roof of the universe;

an eagle hovers over me in the skies,
flapping wings,

shedding colors,
protecting my dreams,

that can never be a part of history,
the world would ever like to write!

Jon Tribble

Pure Gestures

Legal tender, heavy silver
coins, tin crosses on paper-clip chains,
they would hand all of these to us—
    only children—and we'd deliver
our cache to counselors who were trained
to slip back into pockets the straws,
    glass baubles, each sliver of wood,

    and the mentally handicapped
men and women clapped their never-empty
hands and laughed. I learned the rules
    of what and how, why and when
to turn over these gifts of happy
giving, to return each coin, the spools
    of bright thread as seriously

    as each had been given. Father
explained the honest goodwill and cheer
of their presents, said, *We should receive*
    in the same loving spirit, rather
than let greed or mistrust interfere
with the pure gesture. We would
    leave his lecture with a little fear

    and much awe at the innocence
it was now obvious we were all losing.
Pitching horseshoes against the heat, dust
    of Arkansas summer, we'd wince
a bit each time one of them, choosing
to be helpful, ran over to the rusted
    railroad spike we'd been using

in our makeshift pit, picked
up the shoes and returned them, though
the turn wasn't over. It was those
        small acts of gentle wicked
kindness and consideration we found so
annoying, left us wanting to pack clothes
        and possessions, leave home

        for the two weeks beginning
and ending those summer camps, not face
the smiles we knew some day we wouldn't
        return, the prospect of weighing
a coin in the hand, looking both ways,
then stashing it away where we shouldn't,
        finding there was no grace within us

to be any less or more than miserably human.

Martin Willitts, Jr.

The Revolution Came Early
This Winter

*"I can't tell if the day is ending, or the world, or if the secret of secrets is
within me again."*

— Akhimatova

*

There is a darkness upon darkness — some darker
than others, more purple. This is what
it has come to — this lack of seeing, this lack of
shape and dimension, until we wonder,
were we ever here?

Who can admit seeing such a horror?

I can. I have nothing to lose. I have lost everything:
my home: my land; my love;
my love of life.

We are still being erased: memory; belief
in possibilities; kisses smaller than postage stamps;
stamps across the heart like hooves, like bee stings,
like black whips; like crosses burning and crying.

You want me to admit to things that never happened.
You want me to say that horses can pass for nighttime
when you just made me confess there is no daytime.
I can't. You have taught me to say little as possible.

*

55

Silence whispers my name in my ear. It is posted
as being suspicious. If I stay low to the ground
like snow, maybe no one will notice me.
If I wear a shawl of darkness, maybe I can blend in.

There are people taking names, turning them in.
Everyone is afraid. No one knows who to trust.
When they took you away, they destroyed your name
until you wonder if you were ever here, or imagined yourself.

When your name melted in my heart like an icicle,
from faraway your memory found me, even in hiding.
When you came, the room brightened for a second.
Not even the soldiers could drag your memory away again.

*

Who can say what is normal?
Today, a group of soldiers were marching in step
and they had no idea where they were going
or even if they were going in the right direction.

They moved in darkness, fearing darkness,
not realizing they were the darkness.
Darkness was inside their coats, written as love letters
in case something happens. It usually does.

When one man fell behind, he was shot.
He was shot when his boot came loose.
He was shot for thinking he could fix something.
This is what it has come to.

I found his letter. It was to his mother.
He was too young for a girlfriend, barely twelve.
This is what war has come to. He died without knowing
love, or sunshine, or possibilities, or matches.

He died before a beard could cover his freckles.
He bled in the snow, his mouth trying to ask
for his mother, too young to do anything, really.
He died because his boots slowed him down.

When I thought of you, in the unknown,
your name was a swirl of snowflakes.
Do you remember how I unbuttoned your darkness,
kissed your fear and mailed it away?

The last thing you told me when they took you away
was run, run like snow across darkness, run
as if bees were stinging, run until you hear your hooves
as names falling off lists and everyone on it is safe.

I ran invisible, pass soldiers looking for me.
I ran so fast they cannot see my name was fleeing.
I took you with me. I carried you like a baby inside me.
I cried like a soldier singing his own death before a battle.

Now both of us are escaping my dear.
I am going where no one, except you, can find me.
And when I get there, you will be there.
We will huddle together like struck matches.

There will be no more whips, no more madness,
no more mass graves like a pond of winter ducks,
no one searching for us anymore.
There I will be — waiting for you.

Kath Abela Wilson

The Green

It was a tree, becomes a song, a table, leaf after leaf, opening. We sit around its absence as it floats on memory. Shapeshifter becomes dreamcatcher, an escape hatch, small carved windmills turning very fast. We pull up small stumps polished clean.

congress of earthlings
considering the revival
of green
we fall asleep
in different languages

DIANE FRANK

I continue to believe that peace is possible. I believe that each one of us can be an island of peace, giving our gift to the world. In small acts of kindness, like giving food or a care package to a homeless person, we can make the planet better. Even when we feel powerless to change the larger picture, we can continue to be a green tree in a living forest. Poetry, music and art are powerful ways to bless the planet with grace and vision. My prayer is for our planet to survive. I want in all ways to be a blessing.

JP DiBlasi

Au Nom de Père

Death again, in god's name.

Media doesn't show the faces
of the newly dead,
too quickly converted into data anonymity:
numbers lost, attack locations,
three at the stadium, four in restaurants,
the deadliest, a concert, at the Bataclan.

Suddenly, when the bombs exploded
and the world tilted upside down,
I saw everything through the eyes of the dead.

In the grief of Paris, I recalled those who fell
or fled from towers in New York,
those eyes, brown and blue,
returning to me in my dreams.

Daniel J. Langton

Paris at Dusk

I have seen the day away, the man
cutting lamb in a stall, the children
speaking intricate French,
the Seine reminding me it is the blood
that flows inside the city,
the sudden signs.

The light the artists come for
is going, men are flicking their collars,
women hurrying, those Parisian women
who seem to know something
you would give anything to know.

What is it, why is it
when you feel that at any moment
life will arrive? A poster,
music from an open window,
a few drops of rain.
The city will make it happen,
will tell you a secret,
deciding to be a friend.

Mary Kay Rummel

Remembering Paris

When you remember me, conjure Paris—
the clack of high heels striking holes
in the night courtyard below our spiraled stairs.

You won't remember what I wore—
red dress with blue sash.
I remember your French,
voice warm, like a balm,
your eyes that deep end blue
color playing zither on my heart.
I saw the sea in them,
grace light of sun on waves
the shores we would follow.

Night after light filled night we walked
along the Seine with our children—
Timothy talking beside us,
Andrew running ahead, scouting for *glâce.*
After, I lay with my head on your chest.
Even now, some savor of me stays
in Paris clinging to those aureate nights.

KB Ballentine

Planting Bulbs in Winter

Waters froth, surge sand, the rocks,
fields fallow and frozen.
Dreams blurred by groans from Paris,
thunder cracking the Bataclan, Stade de France.
Stores smeared in blues and reds, flashing lights
strobe cars — braised tomatoes, *coq au vin* staining
sidewalks. Flirting lashes, candlelight snuffed,
footsteps stumbling, rushing,
gone.

In the desert, siroccos blow and burn,
but here November spreads cold fingers,
grabs scarves — noose squeezing, city grayed
in static. Beneath the dirt daffodils, lilies
gasp in darkness, air thick as pitch.

Stewart Florsheim

The Best Bread in Montparnasse

After the painting, Le Dejeuner Sur L'Herbe,
by Edouard Manet, 1863

Perhaps she is only a thought:
the man in the black hat
talks about a woman he made love to once
in the Bois de Boulogne
and his friend conjures up her image –
naked, red hair tied back, innocent.

He imagines what she looks like making love,
her eyes half shut, half focused
on her other life:
the long walk alone to her flat
where her husband waits for her,
his disinterest so strong
he drops his Pernod as she walks in.
Or maybe he is with his mistress and the flat is empty,
not quite as cold as if he were in his study
and she lights a fire, pulls out her Flaubert.

The man in the black hat offers
his friend a bunch of grapes and he snaps back
into the conversation: the Impressionist show at the Salon,
the new café on the Blvd. St. Germain.

In the back of his mind, he has decided
that tonight he will visit his mistress
and although she is not well-read,
she bakes the best bread in Montparnasse.
And when he comes over, she will know
to put the bread in the oven and watch it rise,

slowly, as he talks about his morning in the café on the Rue St. Lazare, the afternoon in the park with his friend from the south.

Rachel Landrum Crumble

Black Friday

After Emily Dickinson's "There's a Certain Slant of Light"

I. "There's a Certain Slant of Light"

Late afternoon sun squints
through the west windows.
I am content with leftovers and quiet,
my male child accounted for, and sleeping —
safely home.

II. "Heavenly Hurt, it gives us…"

A distant dog barks without conviction.
Traffic swishes steadily two blocks away.
The last of the gold and scarlet leaves
tumble from the trees.
Protesters in Chicago carry this message
down the Magnificent Mile:
"Justice is the public face of love."
16 shots and Laquan McDonald's
17-year-old life folded like a knife.

III. "None may teach it… —Any—"

A ladybug crawls across the screen, unfolds wings,
flies off. My synapses still smarting
from the 2 a.m. phone call …
felony charge, detention hearing…
Two weeks ago, I told my son, "Be careful
who you get in a car with.
It could cost your very life."

IV. "When it comes, the Landscape listens…"

Today, in Chicago, Paris, and Chattanooga,
shadows held their breath, mourning senseless violence.
Seven shootings in three days in my city alone.
The youngest to die in the Paris attacks was 17.
My son is just that age today.
I exhale. These are reasons why
the heart is convalescent.

Lynn Cohen

Paris

Share with me
my memories of Paris:
a mélange of impressions
indelible painted images
inked in my soul.
I am my own Japanese pillow book.
I wear my words on my skin.
Fragmented mots of tarnished moments
tied together by silver threads
and misted over like the earth
on an early day outing
along the Bois de Boulogne.
Skin taut and pink as the beads
on the necklace you gave me
a Matisse deep pink
on a soon-to-be-distant birthday
so late in life.
I was surprised
I can still feel the dampness
of late spring's longing

Betsy Snider

Paris is Burning

The earth pitches over the edge of time.
Planes disappear behind clouds.
The arc of blue stretches to heaven.

And somewhere far away, bombs explode
light into potsherds of civilization
that drift back into the dust of the universe.

My knees crack, unused to the hard stone
of faith, the sure knowledge of Truth,
the priests chanting in the pines.

I wrap myself in the shroud of doubt
and walk to the lip of the abyss.
Stars shower my shoulders in luminance.

Becky Sakellariou

Hell did not fall out of the sky

after Paris

Hell did not fall out of the sky
this time.

It arrived in human form,
black and furious

aimed at our breasts,
our foreheads, our spirits.

The city wept
trapped inside the evacuation of color.

Blackbirds gathered soundlessly along St. Anthony's
curved gold and marble spires,

our beards turned suddenly gray
like the wasted desert sands.

*

Why, then, was everything I saw today
filled with wonder?

At dusk, water fell from the heavens
and washed the blood

from the bodies, leaving them as if just born,
clean, curled, quiet.

The ribbed clouds released a band of last minute sun
illuminating our wet, scared faces

and a lullaby crept out from
the shattered cobblestones.

Like the trout who thrives not in confinement
but in rushing, roiling currents,

I shall live in the water from now on,
not in the fire.

I may drown, but I will not burn.

Helga Kidder

Je Suis Parisienne

Last stop before *Place Pigalle,* the Metro surfaces
from the city's underworld.

Morning is hopeful. Sun warms pedestrians,
airs comforters and pillows.

A tour guides me to *Sacre Coeur.*
Pray? For whom? You, who machine-gunned
a theater-full of patrons, splattering their lives
like refuse over seats and floor?

To stand helpless. To have to close the door
behind what seemed perfectly good lives.
As if standing at a summit's edge
before letting go for the free fall.

After climbing a thousand steps,
sun lifts fog like a petition off the Seine.
The city mourns ashes but triumphs in light.

Thomas Centolella

After the Latest Disaster

After the latest disaster
visited upon someone who never saw it coming
or saw it but was helpless to stop it

the disaster that visited two someones
a favorite number of disaster

and decided it was still hungry and needed to eat
as much of the world as possible
its appetite was that great

after the damage and the disbelief
after the news feeds that downlinked into adrenalized dreams
after the first responders and the body bags and the clean up crews
there were numbing analyses and breaking updates
and experts going rote in their expensive suits and earnest tones
there were candidates flogging their approval ratings
and eyewitness accounts by those who had to pause
and gather themselves
and apologize for no good reason
before going on

And there were determined assertions
of how to respond
though an adequate response was not given
to everyone visited by the latest disaster

The nightmare racket in the streets
was no more dreadful than the quiet nightmare
at a yellow kitchen table
with its tiny shakers of flavor
and slender vase embracing a solitary flower
its petals fallen in a circle like an omen

And so it went for many hours
for many days
for too many years

The morning after the latest disaster
you woke alone
to the daunting nothing
that is always there
and will not be magicked away

and because your spirit had been extracted
you had to will your body to the brink
of where it attempts to rest and then
to its feet rising as if
you were still yourself

passable impostor

rising routinely as the sun
to the thousand things
you had to do

and which no longer mattered

and which had to be done

Nancy Lee Melmon

Prayer

I'm in a high-rise with glass windows,
and I hear ticking.
Stop the night.
Convince the Earth to halt her rotation.
There is a two year old
sitting next to me, gripping my hand.
A boy with black hair,
and his cheeks are wet.
Abandon your canisters of nerve gas.
Lay them silently on the floor.
Do not touch that wire.
Just cut it.
He is the same age as your son,
who has a different name.
Tilt his chin back;
wipe his nose.
Do you have a magic wand
that will clear this room of shrapnel and clouds?
His heart is beating fast.
Cease and step back.
If you do, this room will stop tilting, and our boys
will keep breathing.

Loretta Diane Walker

50 Boulevard Voltaire

On the day after Armistice Day in 1918,
Monet promised his homeland a "monument to peace"
in the form of massive water lily paintings— Kristy Puchko

Music smells of blood and gunpowder,
tastes like fear's sweat.
November's cold fingers trace shadows
and emptied chambers of inhumaneness;
tears echo on solemn streets.
Red in its liquid sneakers runs over stones and flesh.
Security's ribs crack.

Where is Monet's Paris, with its soft-petal Water Lilies?
This one is splattered with brutalities humans heap
upon other humans. Where is the dignity
in severing *joie de vivre?*
What monument shall we offer
the afflicted, the fragmented, the exiled?

The white Frisbee moon suspended in a sad sky?
The trembling air's plethora of prayers?
A bouquet of compassionate hands?
Wind, do not walk gently on those crushed roads of humanity.

Loretta Diane Walker

Silenced

Perhaps it's stuttering rain against the window, the wet
hymn of hope singing in the chorus of a strong wind,

or maybe it's the small head of a morning glory
peeking through dirt burdened with three years of drought,

or it could be the soft words that have a way of burrowing
through bone and walls we build with past injuries

to reach that one we do not want to lose

that makes me believe I can pump peace
in the violent, blood- lust veins

of nations wanting to rule by silencing the tongue.

Christine Vovakes

Flowers Not Guns

"They have guns but we have flowers."
— A father to his son at a Paris memorial site for victims of the terrorist attack

No battle to match an AK47,
but these petals fuse and form a defense
against the Hun in us. We cluster
and forbid terror's dark ties
to snake through our streets and bind us.

       My child, walk
in this garden, let bee balm
patch your heart.

Evil prances its satyr dance,
but we gather lavender, rose buds and jasmine.
We know evil's soul but won't learn its path
of poisoned briars and twisted tongues.

Cain and Abel opened that gate
and never came home again.

Ellaraine Lockie

Blessings

All of them at Starbucks on Thanksgiving morning
Solo men whose women don't exist
Or are home cooking in concert
with a country of women and a hick town of men

Surrounding families speaking German and Japanese
who will later eat turkey and cranberries
at someone else's house
Secretly wondering why the ballyhoo
The British couple trying not to think too hard
about pilgrims and revolutions
A man wearing an embroidered kufi

Yet why not an international day of gratitude
A day away from differences, right here now
Push tables together, carve up a pumpkin cake
Dress the morning in coffees from other countries
and celebration of the one we're in
Hold hands in a blessing that bars
bloodshed, politics and religion
Cheerio, ohayo, salaam, dankbar

LOIS P. JONES

Now I've been happy lately
Thinking about the good things to come
And I believe it could be
Something good has begun
Oh, I've been smiling lately
Dreaming about the world as one
And I believe it could be
Someday it's going to come

'Cause I'm on the edge of darkness
There ride the Peace Train
Oh, Peace Train take this country
Come take me home again

~ Cat Stevens

Negotiating the produce aisles of my local market as I consider a way toward opening my leaf of the peace anthology, Peace Train rings confidently over the speaker system and I'm immediately transported to 1971 – striped bell bottoms and waist-long hair, afros and peace signs and pre-teen visions of massive protests against the Viet Nam war drifting across our black and white screen. As the agony of an endless conflict raged on, Apollo 14 crew ghost-walked across a pocked surface and planted another American flag on the moon.

In the subsequent decades of upheaval, peace has come to mean so much more than an end to war. The plea for peace is a desire for an end of conflict not only between countries but cultures, religions, genders, races and political ideologies. In our day of sensitivity to all forms of conflict, the question of how we understand one another has never been more urgent.

It's not as if we don't have the answers. Whether we find them through religion, philosophy or the lessons of our ancestors, we can realize universal wisdom and truths. It takes a daily pledge to put what we've learned into practice as we witness injustice, oppression, inequalities and violence in our streets. It takes a storehouse of inner peace to understand intolerance in others and find constructive ways to reconcile our strained relationships.

If the spirit doesn't move us, logic should. One can look to science and observe the ways in which all species of life are interdependent and still we obfuscate truths to justify our actions. If survival is the dynamic word of existence what dictates that urge? Why is there a need to either obliterate or conform our differences? There's no reductive answer. It's not "greed" or "Western beliefs" or "prejudice" or "lust for power" but all of these and more, informing a complex set of webbing through our histories. What serves us is truth. Not the invented truths but those which come from a dedication to and a cognizance of awareness.

A wise observer noted, "reading Joy Harjo's poetry is like being in the presence of the great Chanunpa pipe...only the truth is permitted." If only we could gather across the globe to share its essence. Poetry can and does act as conduit by sharing its smoke-ringed language. Truth is as permeable as life. Sit down and lift these poems to your lips. Let them weave through you like Lynne Thompson's *Raffia*, invoking our own ancestors who *bleed the blood of both aborigine / and Inca* - the indistinguishable breath of our being.

Let these poems of witness inspire you to keep faith in the world. *[I]if the weather is a kaleidoscope/view of our inner life* (Linsteadt), *let us pray for (our) enemies* (Harjo) *in the middle of a snow shield,/Chipped along its western edge* (Tarkovsky). *When our temples are gone may (our) voices be (our) temple* (Pinsky). *These (are) the bells/I would trail searching for you* (Ostler). *Be/safe this day,/friends, don't curl/and don't be killed/not this day, not after* (Berdeshevsky).

Let us (be) called to our kindred on the long shore (Robertson): *Make a stand against the chaos of (our) world, sweeping the beach clean.* (Rogers).

Lynne Thompson

Raffia

To the Igbo, everything is family, everything
is connected, Grandmother explained.
Like the weave of this raffia hat, we intertwine.
See? This is the world to the Igbo.

—Chris Abani

To the Igbo, everything is family, everything—
be it small or grand. Whether you look like
I do or look otherwise; whether you can sing
or have no voice at all. In all of nature—moon
fish, elephant tusks, the silkworm and its
kin—no distinctions
can be made. Those who discriminate bring
dishonor to our house, perpetuate the shame
we never want to admit. When singled out,
we wilt needlessly. Relatively speaking everyone

is connected, Grandmother explained.
We bleed the blood of both aborigine
and Inca. Our imagination doesn't strain
under ice-plains or inside the heat of the Gobi
or any other desert at the thought we all
advance, slow as turtles, but we advance as one.
(And those who cannot must be saved like grains
of rice fallen from the rice-pot. When we refuse,
we're doomed to sever the natural connection
that makes us humane and proves that

like the weave of this raffia hat, we intertwine—
the lock of your blond hair braiding with my
dark lock, your breathing identical to mine.)

Where is there a line separating the clouds
showering our cities? Even the caesura
between twilight and moonshade can't be
assigned with precision. All of history is a sign
that we learn and fail and fail again at the very
same rate. That I hold the tether and decide each
bend in the path your sheep will take. Don't you

see? This is the world to the Igbo.
To think otherwise is to dwell in double doubt.
To live otherwise is to live where there is no
point in leaving your tent. This is not difficult.
This won't fill your basket with kolanut. This
is a story to be read by us all every day. We all
have a grandmother who's confirmed it, so you
cannot say it isn't so. Some young Igbo from
a tribe near your village are awaiting your call.
Their breath is indistinguishable from yours.

Joy Harjo

Conflict Resolution for Holy Beings

I am the holy being of my mother's prayer and my father's song
— NORMAN PATRICK BROWN, DINEH POET AND SPEAKER

1. SET CONFLICT RESOLUTION GROUND RULES:

Recognize whose lands these are on which we stand.
Ask the deer, turtle, and the crane.
Make sure the spirits of these lands are respected and treated with goodwill.
The land is a being who remembers everything.
You will have to answer to your children, and their children, and theirs—
The red shimmer of remembering will compel you up the night to walk the perimeter of truth
for understanding.
As I brushed my hair over the hotel sink to get ready I heard:
By listening we will understand who we are in this holy realm of words.
Do not parade, pleased with yourself.
You must speak in the language of justice.

2. USE EFFECTIVE COMMUNICATION SKILLS THAT DISPLAY AND ENHANCE MUTUAL TRUST AND RESPECT:

If you sign this paper we will become brothers. We will no longer fight. We will give you this land and these waters "as long as the grass shall grow and the rivers run."

The lands and waters they gave us did not belong to them to give. Under false pretenses we signed. After drugging by drink, we signed. With a mass of gunpower pointed at us, we signed. With a flotilla of war ships at our shores, we signed. We are still signing. We have found no peace in this act of signing.

A casino was raised up over the gravesite of our ancestors. Our own distant cousins pulled up the bones of grandparents, parents, and grandchildren from their last sleeping place. They had forgotten how to be human beings. Restless winds emerged from the earth when the graves were open and the winds went looking for justice.

If you raise this white flag of peace, we will honor it.

At Sand Creek several hundred women, children, and men were slaughtered in an unspeakable massacre, after a white flag was raised. The American soldiers trampled the white flag in the blood of the peacemakers.

There is a suicide epidemic among native children. It is triple the rate of the rest of America. "It feels like wartime," said a child welfare worker in South Dakota.

If you send your children to our schools we will train them to get along in this changing world. We will educate them.

We had no choice. They took our children. Some ran away and froze to death. If they were found they were dragged back to the school and punished. They cut their hair, took away their language, until they became as strangers to themselves even as they became strangers to us.

If you sign this paper we will become brothers. We will no longer fight. We will give you this land and these waters in exchange "as long as the grass shall grow and the rivers run."

Put your hand on this bible, this blade, this pen, this oil derrick, this gun and you will gain trust and respect with us. Now we can speak together as one.

We say, put down your papers, your tools of coercion, your false promises, your posture of superiority and sit with us before the fire. We will share food, songs, and stories. We will gather beneath starlight and dance, and

<u>rise together at sunrise.</u>

The sun rose over the Potomac this morning, over the city surrounding
    the white house.
It blazed scarlet, a fire opening truth.
White House, or *Chogo Hvtke*, means the house of the peacekeeper, the
    keepers of justice.
We have crossed this river to speak to the white leader for peace many
    times
Since these settlers first arrived in our territory and made this their place
    of governance.
These streets are our old trails, curved to fit around trees.

3. GIVE CONSTRUCTIVE FEEDBACK:

We speak together with this trade language of English. This trade
language enables us to speak across many language boundaries. These
languages have given us the poets:

Ortiz, Silko, Momaday, Alexie, Diaz, Bird, Woody, Kane, Bitsui, Long
Soldier, White, Erdrich, Tapahonso, Howe, Louis, Brings Plenty, okpik,
Hill, Wood, Maracle, Cisneros, Trask, Hogan, Dunn, Welch, Gould...

The 1957 Chevy is unbeatable in style. My broken-down one-eyed Ford
will have to do. It holds everyone: Grandma and grandpa, aunties and
uncles, the children and the babies, and all my boyfriends. That's what
she said, anyway, as she drove off for the Forty-Nine with all of us in that
shimmying wreck.

This would be no place to be without blues, jazz—Thank you/*mvto* to
the Africans, the Europeans sitting in, especially Adolphe Sax with his
saxophones... Don't forget that at the center is the Mvskoke ceremonial
circles. We know how to swing. We keep the heartbeat of the earth in our
stomp dance feet.

You might try dancing theory with a bustle, or a jingle dress, or with
turtles strapped around your legs. You might try wearing colonization like

a heavy gold chain around a pimp's neck.

4. REDUCE DEFENSIVENESS AND BREAK THE DEFENSIVENESS CHAIN:

I could hear the light beings as they entered every cell. Every cell is a house of the god of light, they said. I could hear the spirits who love us stomp dancing. They were dancing as if they were here, and then another level of here, and then another, until the whole earth and sky was dancing.

We are here dancing, they said. There was no there.

There was no "I" or "you."

There was us; there was "we."

There we were as if we were the music.

You cannot legislate music to lockstep nor can you legislate the spirit of the music to stop at political boundaries—

—Or poetry, or art, or anything that is of value or matters in this world, and the next worlds.

This is about getting to know each other.

We will wind up back at the blues standing on the edge of the flatted fifth about to jump into a fierce understanding together.

5. ELIMINATE NEGATIVE ATTITUDES DURING CONFLICT:

A panther poised in the cypress tree about to jump is a panther poised in

90

a cypress tree about to jump.

The panther is a poem of fire green eyes and a heart charged by four winds of four directions.

The panther hears everything in the dark: the unspoken tears of a few hundred human years, storms that will break what has broken his world, a bluebird swaying on a branch a few miles away.

He hears the death song of his approaching prey:

I will always love you, sunrise.
I belong to the black cat with fire green eyes.
There, in the cypress tree near the morning star.

6. AND, USE WHAT YOU LEARN TO RESOLVE YOUR OWN CONFLICTS AND TO MEDIATE OTHERS' CONFLICTS:

When we made it back home, back over those curved roads
that wind through the city of peace, we stopped at the
doorway of dusk as it opened to our homelands.
We gave thanks for the story, for all parts of the story
because it was by the light of those challenges we knew
ourselves—
We asked for forgiveness.
We laid down our burdens next to each other.

Joy Harjo

Rabbit Is Up to Tricks

In a world long before this one, there was enough for everyone,
Until somebody got out of line.
We heard it was Rabbit, fooling around with clay and the wind.
Everybody was tired of his tricks and no one would play with him;
He was lonely in the world.
So Rabbit thought to make a person.
And when he blew into the mouth of that crude figure to see
What would happen,
The clay man stood up,
Rabbit showed the clay man how to steal a chicken.
The clay man obeyed.
Then he showed him how to steal corn.
The clay man obeyed.
Then he showed him how to steal someone else's wife.
The clay man obeyed.
Rabbit felt important and powerful.
And once that clay man started, he could not stop.
Once he took that chicken, he wanted all the chickens.
And once he took that corn, he wanted all the corn.
And once he took that wife, he wanted all the wives.
He was insatiable.
Then he had a taste of gold and he wanted all the gold.
Then it was land and anything else he saw.
His wanting only made him want more.
Soon it was countries, and then it was trade.
The wanting infected the earth.
We lost track of the purpose and reason for life.
We began to forget our songs. We forgot our stories.
We could no longer see or hear our ancestors,
Or talk with each other across the kitchen table.
Forests were being mowed down all over the world.
And Rabbit had no place to play.

Rabbit's trick had backfired.
Rabbit tried to call the clay man back.
But when the clay man wouldn't listen
Rabbit realized he's made a clay man with no ears

Joy Harjo

Spirit Walking in the Tundra
for Anuqsraaq and Qituvituaq

I fly over the Bering Sea toward Nome.
In the breaking up ice are turquoise lakes
In which I can see the sky.
The cargo load so heavy with human need, it
Vibrates to my bones.
In pockets of marrow are nests of sea birds,
Mothers so protective they will dive humans.
I walk from the plane and am met by an old friend.
We drive to the launching place
And see walrus hunters set out toward the sea.
We swing to the summer camps where seal hangs on drying frames.
She takes me home.
This is what it feels like, says her son, as we walk up tundra,
Toward a herd of musk ox.
There is a shaking, and then you are in mystery.
Little purple flowers come up from the permafrost.
A newborn musk ox staggers around its mother's legs.
I smell the approach of someone with clean thoughts.
She is wearing designs like flowers, and a fur of ice.
She carries a basket and digging implements.
Her smell is sweet like blossoms coming up through the snow.
The spirit of the tundra stands with us, and we collect sunlight together,
We are refreshed by small winds.
We do not need books of history to know who we are
Or where we come from, I tell him.
Up here, we are near the opening in the Earth's head, the place where the
spirit leaves
and returns.
Up here, the edge between life and death is thinner than dried animal
bladder.

94

Joy Harjo

This Morning I Pray for My Enemies

And whom do I call my enemy?
An enemy must be worthy of engagement.
I turn in the direction of the sun and keep walking.
It's the heart that asks the question, not my furious mind.
The heart is the smaller cousin of the sun.
It sees and knows everything.
It hears the gnashing even as it hears the blessing.
The door to the mind should only open from the heart.
An enemy who gets in, risks the danger of becoming a friend.

Margo Berdeshevsky

Again Ahead of April

And we are here as on a darkling plain —Mathew Arnold

still chill, or spring not realized yet
but Easter bombs but tulip yellows

spring with winter's gaping holes in
her side—not murdered like the sudden

sky-fallen geese or starlings
black as charred children

—but daring to show her face
spring, unveiling while the pilot crashes

song high above seeds that insist and flower
blind — crashes what confidence is

left for surety in a sky full of queries: why
is any month as cruel as God?

and the dogwood on our corner
explodes so pink again
this year?

Margo Berdeshevsky

Beyond My Used-up Words . . .

Keening with the fallen.
And that is not enough.

Then how will I sleep or write of herons?
Tides, torn in an angry sea's claw. Stilled

flesh whitening
where the wild orchid rises and withers,

her tiny many mouths along a single stalk—
a chorus — all its stilled children

call for any god to reach them.
Breaths stopped — no whispers left —

and that is not enough.

~

When I see you, my breath tears
there between your bodies.

If I say
what I know of plenty and of empty,
how will I sleep, or dream of herons?

Leaps cut down
curled— used— on the bright,
of road blood stilled in its breeze.

Be
safe this day,
friends, don't curl

and don't be killed
not this day, not after. There will be
cold wakings when your fist will haunt all

sleep. When the dun silence will leave.
I mean to see you
if ever I cannot stand.

This side of the new-born stream
there's no blood yet.

But let our cry
carry.
Infant, in its clairvoyant's caul.

Let our knowing—bleed.
How can we sleep, or write of the fallen?

I am without skin
today.
Your drum—deeper, and going deeper in.

And that is not enough.

There is a place where the wing tears.
And there is a day when the heron stands.
And there is a river for revolution

—the hardest love, coming in.
Bring me to the river where lives begin, where
our nakedness needs no skin, bring me to

where it begins and begins. Nameless. And coming in.
At the end of the beginnings, we dress in long light—

a hybrid body of stars—River, where the parched

heart drinks her fill,
hill where the unborn
climb

~

George Jisho Robertson

Stone Ocean Wave

All that long night pebbles roared deep–
Our knees wet, our lips salt
Slipping sliding falling

Pebble shaped the human hand:
The pigments and textures cry for
Earth's ancient pangs

You kissed the stone and the stone sang:
In the rise and fall of your voice
It rose & fell, dissolving to here, eroding to now

My dearest Wave, white-robed and elegant,
We called to our kindred on the long shore:
All who rise and fall here, driven, glistening, calling

Robert Pinsky

Light

(After the Hebrew of Chaim Nachman Bialik)

Not rented not bought not stolen
Not borrowed, my light
Didn't come to me by luck
Or in a rich father's will:

Waiting its time, hidden,
Stubborn little light, as if
Hammered from living rock
I quarried out of myself—
Not much, maybe, but mine
Down to the bone.

When the rock shatters,
It flashes vanishing
Sparks for these verses
I make out of blood and air
And bits of marrow fire.

Robert Pinsky

Stupid Meditation on Peace

Insomniac monkey-mind ponders the Dove,
Symbol not only of Peace but sexual
Love, the couple nestled and brooding.

After coupling, the human animal needs
The woman safe for nine months and more.
But the man after his turbulent minute or two

Is expendable. Usefully rash, reckless
For defense, in his void of redundancy
Willing to death and destruction.

Monkey-mind envies the male Dove
Who equally with the female secretes
Pigeon milk for the young from his throat.

For peace, send all human males between
Fourteen and twenty-five to school
On the Moon, or better yet Mars.

But women too are capable of Unpeace,
Yes, and we older men too, venom-throats.
Here's a great comic who says on our journey

We choose one of two tributaries: the River
Of Peace, or the River of Productivity.
The current of Art he says runs not between

Banks with birdsong in the fragrant shadows—
No, an artist must follow the stinks and rapids
Of the branch that drives the millstones and dynamos.

Is peace merely a vacuum, the negative
Of creation, or the absence of war?
The teaching says Peace is a positive energy.

Still something in me resists that sweet milk,
My mind resembles my restless, inferior cousin
Who fires his shit in handfuls from his cage.

Robert Pinsky

In The Coma

My friend was in a coma, so I dove
Deep into his brain to word him back. I tried

To sing *Hallelujah, I Just Love Her So* in
Ray Charles's voice. Of course the silence grew.

I couldn't sing the alphabet song. My voice
Couldn't say words I knew: *Because I Could
Not Stop For Death, He Kindly Stopped For Me.*

I couldn't remember the Dodgers and the Giants.

I tried to tell him the stories he and I
Studied when we were young. It was confused,
The Invisible Man was laughing at how a man
Felt History jump out of his thick fair head
And beat him half to death, as being the nightmare
Out of which Isaac Babel tried to awake.

The quiet. *Next time won't you sing with me.*
Those great diminished chords: *A girl I know.*

The cold of the coma, lightless. The ocean floor.

I struggled to tell things back from decades gone.
The mournful American soldier testifying
About My Lai: *I shot the older lady.*

Viola Liuzzo, Spiro Agnew, Jim Jones.

And by the time I count from one to four
I hear her knocking. Quiet of the deep,
Our mouths are open but we cannot sing.

Robert Pinsky

Góngora: Life is Brief

Bullets don't fly to the target any quicker,
A war-wagon's wheels muffled by the sand
Don't churn around a corner any quieter,
Than life quickly, quietly comes to its end.

Is anybody stupid enough to doubt it?—
Repeatedly, every day, the rising sun
Warns you: *Life passes, you're a falling comet.*
And every day it leaves the sky dark again.

Carthage gives witness only a fool ignores.
Don't waste yourself on shadows. Hours you abuse
Won't ever be forgiven— these easy hours,

This file of hours that scrape away the days,
These unforgivable days that open and close
One after another and swallow up the years.

Robert Pinsky

Samurai Song

When I had no roof I made
Audacity my roof. When I had
No supper my eyes dined.

When I had no eyes I listened.
When I had no ears I thought.
When I had no thought I waited.

When I had no father I made
Care my father. When I had no
Mother I embraced manners.

When I had no friend I made
Quiet my friend. When I had no
Enemy I opposed my body.

When I had no temple I made
My voice my temple. I have
No priest, my tongue is my choir.

When I have no means fortune
Is my means. When I have
Nothing, death will be my fortune.

Need is my tactic, detachment
Is my strategy. When I had
No lover I courted my sleep.

Arseny Tarkovsky (1907-1989)

Field Hospital

Translated from the Russian by Boris Dralyuk and Irina Mashinski

They turned the table to the light. I lay
Upside down, like meat slapped onto a scale;
My soul swayed, dangling on a string.
I saw myself from the side:
Balanced without makeweights
Against a fat mass from the market.
This
Was in the middle of a snow shield,
Chipped along its western edge,
Surrounded by icy swamps,
By trees on broken legs,
And railroad halts with their skulls
Cracked open, looking black
Beneath their snowy caps, some double,
And some triple.

Time stopped that day,
Clocks didn't run – the souls of trains
No longer flew along the mounds,
Lightless, on grizzled fins of steam.
No gatherings of crows,
No blizzards, no thaws in that limbo
Where I lay naked in disgrace,
In my own blood, outside the pull
Of future's gravity.

But then it shifted, circling on its axis –
The shield of blinding snow.
A wedge of seven airplanes
Turned low above me. And the gauze,
Like tree bark, stiffened on my body,
While someone else's blood now ran

Into my veins out of a flask, and I
Breathed like a fish tossed on the sand,
Gulping the hard, earthy, mica-like,
Cold, and blessed air.

My lips were chapped, and then,
They fed me with a spoon, and then,
I couldn't recall my name,
While King David's lexicon
Awoke upon my tongue.

Then
Snow melted away, and early spring
Stood on her toes and wrapped
The trees with her green kerchief.

1964*

Translator's Note

On translating Arseny Tarkovsky's Field Hospital.

Our goal was to convey the novelty and unique charisma of Tarkovsky's
voice, so apparent to a Russian reader and yet so difficult to reproduce.
Tarkovsky's themes may seem trite at first blush. We tried to preserve
the poem's airy, gestalt-like texture, as well as its hypnotic rhythm and
tone; its interplay of motion and motionlessness; its carefully chosen
verbs, which construct a planetary model of sorts, with the narrator as the
center of a revolving snowy sphere. The first line must be as memorable
as the original, positioning the operating table in immobile cosmic
emptiness. In Tarkovsky's poetic world, enjambments mark key inflexions,
and we kept their tonal and stanzaic position. In stanza four, we sought
a new sense of impetus, which resets the narrator's world in motion.
Tarkovsky's vocabulary is consistent. While translating "Field Hospital",
we imagined we were rendering a whole collection, marking key elements
repeated throughout his poems – words like "mica-like", "blessed", "cold"
– both common and rare, but belonging to "Tarkovsky's lexicon". The
sound "shch" is unusually abundant in the poem; it is associated with the
image of wartime destruction and the swishing sound of cosmic coldness.
In the final lines, it disappears, leaving us with images of earthly beauty.
The word "жирный" is important: we chose "mass" over "weight," because
the former represents weight, and ushers in planetary connotations;
it is also physiological, in a Tarkovskian way ("Кухарка жирная у
скаред..."). We were tempted to use a neologism for "слепительный"
– say, "blistening" – that would combine "blinding" and "glistening", as
in the original, and suggests the soldier's blistered lips. But this "neon"
neologism is atypical for Tarkovsky's diction. And "dazzling", though it
echoes with "blizzard", would not be Trakovsky's word either. We chose
"blinding" as it seemed fresh and suggestive enough in English.

~ Boris Drayluk and Irina Mashinsky

Susan Rogers

Manzanar

"We all need to see hope in the blue sky."
—Kōō Okada

Close your eyes. Imagine the small, clear, two-
paned window of a plane. Through the window you see
a vast expanse of clouds and sky. Each white shape
adjusts itself as if alive. They drift and swim in a field
of blue so beautiful you lift in flight. Our
world is full of poetry. Behind dark skies, hope

dances like clouds in wind. We all need to see hope
in the blue sky. Once monk and poet Thich Nhat Hanh gave two
tangerines to his friend Jim, who paid no attention and devoured
them, missing each orange globe. Hanh thought he had wasted both. "See
and eat your tangerine," he told Jim, giving him a third. "Feel
the fruit." Jim took each section, admired its shape,

tasted the tang upon his tongue. In this way, he made the shape
and flavor real. Years later, Jim languished in a prison cell, hope-
less, crazed with grief. His crime: he refused to fight. He didn't feel
the Vietnam War was right. His path was peace. Heartsick, he sent word to
Thich Nhat Hanh. Hanh's postcard reply asked him to see
confinement differently. "Jim, you're still eating your tangerine." "Our

lives are like tangerines, Hanh said. "With twenty-four sections, or hours.
We need to eat them well." In Manzanar, Henry Fukuhara changed shapes
of confinement into watercolor imagery. He looked deeply until he could see
artistry in clouds of dust, a mountain range, the desert camp where hope
reclaimed lost dignity. Behind barbed wire he found freedom to
imagine life differently. He captured beauty in water, color. We feel

the heart of Manzanar through his resolve to change his world, feel
strokes of light inside the dark. His watercolors blur, dance. Even guard towers
come alive. When Fukuhara looked at a scene he summoned courage to
"change it all around" He asked, "How can I make shapes
different than they are?" He told students, "Step back and see." He hoped
they could "let the big shapes thrive," could see

an entire path when only two bricks were found. "We just need to see
the larger view." Even after going blind, Fukuhara could feel
all things: water, ground, clouds, sky have shape. And hope
too has one if we look for it. Fukuhara still paints peace into our
shadowed lives by perceiving light in each detail, infusing shape
with an artist's braille, reminding us to savor scenes like tangerines, to

eat our moments well and to have a larger view. In Manzanar, we see
peace comes when we close and open our eyes. Behind dark cloud shapes,
hope rises in a sea of wind, dances in a sky blue field.

Susan Rogers

The Tokugawa Kimono
for Kōtama Okada

His father was an Oda; his mother, Tokugawa. He inherited the blood-steeped past of both. But his heart held light. His mission: to rewrite the warrior world into peace. In the Japanese Collection at the Pacific Asia Museum there is a child's kimono with his family crest displayed in a long, clear case. The crest on the silk kimono reminds me of my fighting thoughts: the car that sliced in front of me today, the woman at the bank who stole my place in line. But I remember Kōtama who placed the Oda and Tokugawa crests on the fence of his house in Atami so he would never forget his past, nor judge the conflict he saw in others. Every day he would bow before that fence and practice humility, offering apology for his ancestors. We are all children of warriors. We are all children of light.

The image on the child's kimono suggests fidelity. An old man at the water's edge rakes sand. The old woman next to him holds a broom. Together they make a stand against the chaos of their world, sweeping the beach clean.

at the water's edge
a child digs a moat in sand
over and over

Stephen Linsteadt

What is the meaning of drought,

I wonder, as if the weather is a kaleidoscope
view of our inner life, where vapor trails

pose as clouds in that mocking way
propaganda crisscrosses through bigotry and riots.

What does it mean when reservoirs are empty
and only hope resides on barren shores?

Perhaps drought is the absence of compassion
the view through hungry eyes, our thirst

the bareness of our excuses distilled
into the essentials of what we tolerate:

what our heart knows to be true versus
what our mind refuses to see.

When empathy goes into action kindness condenses
across the jet stream and turns to rain.

Lin Ostler

Soundings

I would not cart a hunting blind
to your waters, nor lodge
a clandestine platform in a tree,
distracted as I would become
by all those blue or green herons,
the avocets or long-billed curlews,
their ochre beaks arcing up, or down.

I'd be tempted to lean out,
stand full-facing, risk the snap
that strews the lot of them to the skies.
If I were stalking your depths
I would not go where you are
but where you have been

the places that drew out
the groan, the awe-struck gasp,
where you went to weep
or stretch out in the sun.

To track your intentionally strewn crumbs
would profit me nothing.
Instead
I'd tease out the stones
you gathered as a child, the bones

you cashed away from animals —
tiny ones like seahorse wings
or the shells from the hermit crabs
you followed home.
These would be the bells
I would trail searching for you.

And if I knew
you were already gone such a great distance
that I would never find you,

I would take those infinitesimal wing struts,
the cochlear sound of shells,
the resonance of ropes rasping
against the rim of a coracle
irretrievably out to sea,

and string together the menagerie
that only I could understand,
affix my final shard beneath its clasp

and watch it sink
into the immeasurable beauty
of the tidal pool at my feet.

Joy Harjo

Sunrise Healing Song

Shining persons arrive here
Ha yut ke lani
Open your being
Ha yut ke jate
In every small thought of what to fix
In every immense thought of dancers winding through the
 Milky Way
Ha yut ke lvste
What obscures, falls away.
Ha yut ke hutke

RUSTIN LARSON

"I release you, my beautiful and terrible
fear."
—Joy Harjo

Who do we think we are, anyway, we poets in search of peace? Our enemies and detractors would say we are all wasting our time, that the die is cast, that peace is not the nature of life on earth, get used to it.

But wait! Did I use the word "enemies?" Who are these anti-peace monsters?

You are white so you can't possibly understand me.
You are brown so you can't possibly understand me.
You are Hindu so you can't possibly understand me.
You are Christian so you can't possibly understand me.
You are straight so you can't possibly understand me.
You are gay so you can't possibly understand me.
You are female so you can't possibly understand me.
You are male so you can't possibly understand me.
You are young so you can't possibly understand me.
You are old so you can't possibly understand me.
You are rich so you can't possibly understand me.
You are poor so you can't possibly understand me.
You are native born so you can't possibly understand me.
You are an immigrant so you can't possibly understand me.
You are an atheist so you can't possibly understand me.
You are a believer so you can't possibly understand me.

As the ancient comic strip *Pogo* is often quoted, "We have met the enemy and he is us."

If you can see the river running through our words you can hear our common mind. We have each an awareness. Each awareness is in the end the same awareness. Vasudhaiva Kutumbakam. The world is my family. The earth is one organism and these bodies belong to it. Subtract our bodies and we are the same light. Our earthly bodies share a common ancestry, and so do our souls.

History is remembering, but it can also be a catalyst for radical forgetting or forgiving.

We can remember, but we can also release. We can release the legacy of being the descendants of thieves and murderers. We can also release the legacy of being the descendants of victims.

"Oh, you have choked me, but I gave you the leash.

You have gutted me but I gave you the knife.

You have devoured me, but I laid myself across the fire." —Joy Harjo

Let us go forward in peace.
Sincerely,
Rustin Larson

Paul Stokstad

Poem with Five Titles

In my poem
with five titles
I'll start off with

The Declaration of Incompetence

I already wrote an essay called
The Declaration of Interdependence
Modeled after the original

But that was when I was being nice
Since what I really wanted to write
Was the Declaration of Incompetence

And in my poem with five titles
I will declare the incompetence
Of the US government
to protect anyone from any single terrorist

since, as we know, they are creating terrorists
faster than they are eliminating them.

I'll declare their incompetence
To create peace

Since they are flat out ignorant
About peace, and haven't a clue
As to how to create it
Unless you think that going to war
Is a great place to start

And let's also note

That they do not revere
Celebrate, remember or pay
Anyone who ever stood up, lay down
Or sat in for peace.

I'll also declare their incompetence
To represent the best aspects of the American people
Since they are so good, right now, at delivering the
Most obvious, jingoistic, narrow, and
counterproductive responses to world events
That could ever have been imagined.

I will also declare now and forever the incompetence
Of the both the fundamentalist Christians
And the Jihadist Islamics
In their relationship to God.

I understand that they believe in God.
But I don't think that they are getting close to God,
Seeing God, or becoming more Godly.

At the root, these religions are failing to connect
Themselves to God in any real way.
And therefore, they are incompetent

And are relying on the tiniest possible scope
Of human, not divine comprehension,
When they go out to kill and die for God
Who, as we have established, they neither
Know or connect with

I tell you, you are no good at
what you think you are good at.
And your religion sucks, since, as we have seen,
it is not working.

Fix that, and then we'll talk

I'll also declare the incompetence
Of our educational system
That can create good working
But not enlightened citizens,

A legal system that punishes
But doesn't prevent crime,

And a medical profession
That catches the fallen
But is blind to the fall

Then, in my five title poem
For peace

I'll use the second title,

Passive Fist

Where I'll explain how
Peace is not just some sort of quiet
Time between wars

But is actually the deep, profound silence
With burgeoning, infinite power
On the surface of which
A million atomic bombs,
Exploding, all at once

Is just a whisper
Barely noticeable
In the vast cosmic array
Which is its expression
And it's completely dependent
Slightly decayed, derivative,
Merely apparent epiphenomenon
In every virtual second

Or nanosecond

In this peace, your war in Iraq, your world wars,
your thousands of wars in human history
are lightly blown ripples in a silent pool

This is the peace that we have
Behind us, to counteract
The warring tendencies
in our little world today

This is the peace that is available
To make war into
an old, cruel, tired joke,
No longer in circulation.

This is the peace that we can rub
All over the faces of these so-called
Realists, and say, your military solution
Is not now and never has been realistic

Never once in history has a war caused peace.

Why should the fact
that you are completely ignorant of that
make things any different this time?

Those that do not learn from history
Are condemned not only to repeat it
But to become it

Hear me, I hold a flower
In my passive fist
So tightly

You cannot unclench this hand
You cannot stop this peace
You cannot sanely laugh

And belittle
the power
of this passive fist

And yet the flower I hold
Is still planted in good soil
And is delicately growing to the sky

Then, in my
poem with five titles
I'll handle that pesky Iraq question, with the simple title:

I say we walk.

I say we walk out of Iraq and don't look back.

I say we admit that we were wrong
And simply, one night, all disappear.
Take the planes, leave the tanks,
take the soldiers,
And simply go.

I don't really care if Iraq has a democratic government or not
I don't really care if Iraq has an Islamic government or not
Or even if Iraq gets Saddam back.

None of that matters to me.

I just don't want another American
In or out of uniform
To get shot or beheaded or simply blown up
doing what shouldn't have been done
in the first place, nor do I want any

Iraqi Islamic Jihadist or even Al Qaeda
to get killed either

Let them have their religion.

Let them have their country

They didn't attack us.
We don't need to be attacking
Or, at this point, protecting them

I say we walk
And let them sort it out.

There will be no loss of pride, I assure you.
It is now long since gone.

Then, in my poem of five titles, I'll say:

Never Again.

Never again,
once we have cleaned up
this ridiculous Neocon
administration and
kicked the religious right back
To the last pew
where they belong,
with the other
Reformed alcoholics
And everyone else who
Looks at an intelligent man
With suspicion

Never again
Will we be sleeping and
Let such backward, boorish, and
Blunt people get in power

Never again will we be the
Brusque, brutish, bully of the world
Never again will we
wander around

Having fun and
making what money we can
while these primitive types
plot and scheme their way into place

never again
you see, because
as the last title
in my poem with five titles,

I'll use a silent title
That no one can hear
But the effect of this phrase

Will be that I will be
In my own life
As if a radio
broadcasting peace

Because I am so full
Of peace, made of peace,
Living peace, being peace
Feeling, tasting,
Brimming over and radiating
infinite peace

And then I will be doing the only thing
I can truly do for peace

Not just voting for some
peace candidate
Once every four years

Only to have my vote wiped out by someone else
Who is at war with themselves and others

Not arguing positions of international affairs
and economic policy

not really being part of the
governmentalist view
of human happiness

such as democracy, the cure for everything
and by the way, could we put a pipeline here?

Just me,
being the peace
Knowing the peace,
Radiating infinite peace,

In this, the section of the poem
With the silent title
You, too, could ask yourself
How am I feeling, right now,
Right here...

Do I feel peace?
Am I at peace?

Is every ounce of my body
My mood, my feelings
My mind, my soul,
My heart, my life
Brimming with
blissful peace

You could ask
Am I part of the peace
Or a piece of the war.

Join me, now
In doing the one thing that you can do
Not once every four years
Not just another vote

In creating peace
In your own world
24/7, every second, every hour
every day of every year

join me in the silent
peaceful title
of this poem

it's the least that you can do
it's the most that you can do

it's the most
being that all you can be.

Be the piece of society
That is being the peace
Be the being
that is being the peace

Be the silent title of this poem
With me
Let's all, together,
Be the peace
That wants to be.

Note: Written during the US war in Iraq.

Robert Schultz

Vietnam Veterans Memorial, Night

To the left the spotlit Washington Monument
Jabs the air, progenitive, white;
Beyond trees, to the right, the stonework glows
Where Lincoln broods in his marble seat;

And here, between, in the humid dark,
Where curving pathways lead and branch,
Sally and I step forward carefully
Somewhere near the open trench.

Choppers shuttle across the sky
With jets for National crying down,
But we've lost our way. The intricate dark
In the center of town moves all around.

There are others here: white T-shirts drift
In heavy air. Then three bronze soldiers
Caught in floodlights across the field
Stare hard at where we want to go.

From above we find the wall's far end
And begin to descend. Ahead of us
Soft footlights brush the lustered stone,
Dim figures trace their hands across

The rows of letters, and others, hushed,
File past in the dark. At first we are only
Ankle deep in the names of the dead,
But the path slopes down. Quietly,

We wade on in. In the depths beside
The lit inscription, men and women

130

Hold each other, mortal, drowning.
Many have stopped at a chosen station

To touch an absence carved away.
From deep inside the chiseled panels
Particular deaths rush out at them.
The minds of veterans gape like tunnels

To burning huts. We are over our heads.
Now Sally turns, sobs hard, and stops.
We cling to each other like all the rest
And climb away with altered steps.

Ken Chawkin

Sanctifying Morning

Charcoal in a church,
Incense-filled smoke,
Knees on the ground,
Wafer on a tongue —
Prayers ascend the sky.

It's Sunday morning,
And I have my own rituals.
The smell of burnt toast sanctifies the morning air.
Orange rinds round out the debris of breakfast.
Fumes float upwards from a hot coffee cup.

Having pacified the body's urges,
With no work to be done today,
Though the senses focus outward,
It's time to bring them within,
And prepare for this peaceful morning.

I retire to my meditation room,
Sit comfortably, and close the eyes.
Thinking my mantra, effortlessly,
I descend to the depths of my mind,
And transcend.

My body follows —
Breath slows, and suspends,
Heart beats quieter,
Brain cells speak softly, in unison —
I'm at peace with myself.

This is the true communion of the spirit
Within the church of the Self.
No pews are required here
As one prepares to meet the maker
Of one's life.

Nynke Passi

The Morphology of Compassion
& Indifference

Gusts of wind rough up the white hibiscus on the lawn.
Petals tear. The sky looks sad enough to rain.

Leaves rustle requiems for flimsy bird bones
& under a sleeping pigeon's wing huddles a sliver of silence.

Vincent van Gogh wrote to his brother, Theo: *There is peace*
even in a storm. The heart of man, like the sea, hides storms, tides & pearls.

•

Why does the sea beat itself senseless on rock? Eternity drips
like a leaky faucet. God & little blossom trees bravely try

to manufacture beauty—whether fine art or
cheap mimicry. But look at van Gogh, Pound, Plath:

passion is dangerous business & can induce lunacy.
Akira Kurosawa said, *In a mad world, only the mad are sane.*

Shadow soils the air's gown. Is there no soap
strong enough to wash out darkness? The moon,

like an Afghan woman, wraps up in thin blue veils.
If the sun covered her face like that, it would always be night.

•

Prayers burn deep inside the throat like votives.
Identity is a peg on which we hang our time.

Plumber Juan Ruiz was arrested in Spain for charging
to keep the devil out of people's sinks & drains.

Souls bend easily like coat hangers. Dreams are pollen,
their weight nearly imagined. People collect love

like lint, then throw love out, even if it sticks.
Bodies can't stop playing dress-up with dust.

•

Is there a language untouched by hate?
Who hears the apology of the rain,

the pizzicato of spider feet playing cobweb harps
up in heaven near the ceiling?

Who notices that grasshoppers pray summer sacred
or that pebbles are soft like a child's wrist?

•

The sun's lips kiss earth goodbye so fervently they bleed.
The moon rises, a dispassionate saint.

Chinese poet Li Po, journeying by boat, tried to kiss
the moon's perfect reflection, fell overboard & drowned.

Unflinchingly, the lepidopterist sticks pins through butterflies.
Clouds keep mounting each other, procreating like rabbits.

Dwell on the beauty of life, said Marcus Aurelius. *Watch
the stars & see yourself running with them.*

But though stars sparkle with glory, they are dead
& don't know anyone's story.

Paradox operates on the same finely crafted hinges
as books & butterfly wings, opening inside out.

Suzanne Rhodenbaugh

Grasp of Islam

The woman lay on a hard narrow bed,
head and torso slightly raised. When a they
removed her veil, small forests were growing
on her face, divided by plains
where the veil had been. I took this as a sign
the veil was good. Then God,
who had no person, began to hand down
bottles of milk. I took this to be
manna from heaven.
Then I thought to call
the forests of her face
oases.

Suzanne Rhodenbaugh

The Dogs of September

In Cherokee legend, animals and people talked
until a chasm came between. Then the dogs dwelt
with the animals, which they understood they were,
yet looked with longing across. And just before the divide
could no longer be breached, leapt – only they,
out of all the animals on earth – to the people's side.

Maybe some rescuer told this to his shepherd,
who listened out of love and trust. And maybe the dog's spirit,
fallen at the crush of the dead,
did rise, and he went to try again to find the life

in that hole of hurt. The man himself needed succor,
and so trusted the goodhearted innocent beast,
who led him through the ruinage wrought by human ardor
that year on the eleventh of September.

Suzanne Araas Vesely

World Peace

…has always been here:
emerging when it can.
But not as the politicians would have it.
Not as history books spin the story.
No treaties end divisions.
No speeches move peace any closer.
No law created ever makes it happen.
Looking back: they only made things worse.
How the Berlin wall came down:
someone just brought a hammer, and a chisel.
A soldier decided to help.
Then another.
Nothing was negotiated. Nothing signed. Nothing spoken.
Even words in a poem just return empty-handed, but there is that quiet
resonance that it recalls…
that Something out of reach of mere words.
There it is. Whole. Complete.
Suddenly all those snakes
are only quivering shadows.
A city doomed to a long, hot summer
blazes with love and light instead.
And no one seems to know why.
A young street lord on a hit list in Colombia
ends up in my library
assembling that ill-fated study carrel donation in half an hour,
with its thousand tiny pieces and no instructions.
It had baffled us all for a year.
You learn to think fast in those places.
Sometimes a thought can turn around in mid-course, and everything changes.
Children of ethnic cleansing
finding lost joy.
Their mothers, remembering to live,

begin again, after a long and painful silence, to sing.
Bullies and toadies you have known
no longer haunt your nights, or the nights of your neighbors on this
planet.
Guns are for sale, but no one needs or wants them.
Rain comes in time. Everyone is full.
The earth grows purer, washed clean.
Riches all calculated in degrees of happiness instead of holdings.
This is not fantasy. It is inevitable.
Peace or fear: they always come from within,
But peace emerges from the place within where
there is a silence that roars out creation.
You can see the music. You can hear in it
the sound of empty hospitals,
whales dancing, tygers reach for their bows of burning gold,
away from analysis, free at long last.
You begin to remember when every religion breathed eternal life.
The Sacred, that was once found everywhere.
That time is here for you.
It is waiting.

R. Steve Benson

Things To Do When You Live
On the Wrong Side Of The Tracks

Switch stations. Eat sadness sandwiches
while cheering brooms and witches
sliding along smooth handles...

Floss. Jog. Welcome wet dogs
with physics until prickly hairs
cha-cha-cha on necks of love.

Laugh lathering with velvety mud.
Skip feuds. Swap fluids. Scan
scars too deep to fade or forget.

Salute Losers. Recruit trees. Seek
knees, thighs all the way up to sighs.
Odds are you're in for a sweet surprise.

You crave the crisp weeping of wounds,
bloody tracks from notched wooden spoons
reaching back to mix itches with scratches.

You need a good drenching in cold rains
while trains of thoughts reach batches
of depots of doubt under dream steam.

To make a herd I heard you need two
cowed cows wading knee deep through
purple thistles in udder bliss.

R. Steve Benson

Feet

(after "Hands" by Donald Justice)

No longer can the feet stand
The stinking prisons of shoes.

Sometimes they slap at wet wood
Like fish dying on a dock.

Sometimes they act like weapons
Kicking bodies of water.

Formerly there were sisters
To trip, bare races to run.

If now their toes become traps,
All their targets are local.

They dream of never slipping
Under tongues in rooms of shoes.

They think of leaving clear prints
In the mud of the future

Where all of their ancestors
Step together from the past.

As their soles grow thin on earth
Think of the feet as leaving,

As dancing away. Think of
The emptiness of the shoes.

Bill Graeser

Of Mothers and War

I often think it is the mothers
who should decree when and if
we go to war—who would know
better to protect?

Wearing an apron, ladle in hand,
let the Generals knock at their
porch door before deploying
in Nam, Afghanistan, Iraq.

In the making of life, men give
only their semen—that they so
like to give—while women give
nine months of their blood

and their body as cradle, then
launch in repeated pain-thrust
a child between their knees.
Yes, let Congress, the Pentagon

and the blood-smeared stockholders
of war turn to the mothers,
and if even for the first time—
let them do as mother says.

S. Stephanie

Franz Wright asks "What do you see yourself doing in 10 minutes?"

Sitting on the edge of my chair, unbuttoning my chest
and watching the shipwreck of my culture pass through.
How the news drones on as another captain jumps

into the latest Grand Old Party's boat, then threatens
to sue when the scandal of his pedophilia costs him the election.
I'll want to get up and go to the corner store where they have red slushes

and an ATM that charges me twice. Sometimes three times! I see
where they were robbed again last night. I'm not afraid of guns. I'm terrified
of the people behind them. I wish I could go back to my old job

at the bookstore, but it's gone virtual and I don't know how to swim
through ether. How Queequeg would hate it here.
I wish I could write the novel that convinces everyone

to go back to their childhoods, embrace Popeye
and Bluto, go on, get down and sentimental
even if it means licking the cream out of the Oreos.

In other words, in 10 minutes, I'll continue
building that boat of my dreams. The one that skims
over these oceans brimming with oil and needles.

What else is there to do? Now that we have allowed
a mockery of Melville's fathomless seas
made a buffoonery of Whitman and his green grasses?

W. E. Butts

Primary

What then of snow and ice, the troubled
wind? Wrens perch on bare branches
or swoop for suet. We all have needs.

The politicians gone, again we're back
in a state of grace. Our nominated differences
and collective selves reside in places lit
by what we've come to believe:

Something certain as granite
must hold us. Weather reminds us
we too will settle.

Denis Stokes

Tasting Africa

I am tasting Africa—Yergacheffe in this café,
This young woman's eyes, silver, a skin all pearl
And her hair a brown river through a wilderness
Of dream. I am tasting Africa with this scone,
Listening to a speech I read at fifteen for no particular
Reason—Haile Selasse. The coffee is deep, rich and dark
But a touch dry on the surface.
I lift my cup as one might lift the weight of slaves.

I am tasting Africa, Mzuzu of the highlands, orphans
Clapping in the backstreets of Ekwendeni, the ground rooted
Expanse of wind across the Nyika of swiftfootedness
And the graced canopies of brachystegia. I am tasting
The kiln fires of Dedza, the bittersweet chalk of the technical college
In Lilongwe, the blue of Cape Maclear like a kid's freezie,
Bright deep blue from Livingstonia to the Chipome Valley
As I gaze back, below- throat gulping at the Lake of Stars.
I am tasting Africa, Harry's Bar, Carlsberg, Carlsberg,
Huche Kuche and goat's head and roast chicken, meals
Prepared by Tami—sheer selfless, self-filling art,
The blood of Chilembwe and the marble dust at the monument
Of Hastings Kamuzu Banda, on the way to the airport
Along the winter dry Kamuzu Road. I am tasting
The dew I was then, as visitor, perhaps friend and in the dewdrops,
Quarrels. I am almost tasting the mvuu farting, assured
In pure presence: *this is my territory*, crocodiles, fish hawks
All quarter and respect... Shire River of ghosts and bones.

I am tasting Africa and I have stopped dreaming:
No Kim Bassinger or Meryl Streep waiting beside
Some dangerous Serengeti, no Peck or Jaluka waiting
On the peaks of Kilamanjaro crying out 'sing your song'.

I am singing of Africa, the song in my ear an unsung song.
I am tasting Kenyan coffee, *President's Choice,* purchased
Unlike, I confess, my normal OFT...praying to Kenyatta—
A name muttered with reverence by Father Quinn once, petty
And effeminate, as he wept openly before us,
Having returned '71, from Biafra...They cry, they cry:

The heart's dark in London, the darkening heart
Of Ottawa, Antwerp, Amsterdam and Washington-
The beloved countries of lost tribal lines and fires...
Bantu, Chichewa, Tonga, Ngoni. I am tasting Africa, pray
To Dallaire and to my friend, once a Shell corporation lawyer, half
Saint now, one with nature, whom I forgive as I read
Soyinka, Walcott looking back in hunger, Arthur Nortje
Blown out like a quick match in a damp wind, the water jars
Borne like dreams of children carried by graceful, draped women.
I am tasting Africa, remembering Nairobi six months ago,
The drying streams near the gaping silos, the carvings sold
In the airport- half Indiana Jones, half Bogart, the bottled
Water, coffee beyond description, the carved giraffes and
Cold Tusker under low ceilings. I am tasting Africa and it is
Good—bloodroot, red bush, high ground, patient wind,
The sun above diamond glint in the crow's eyes- hard and long.

Paula Yup

World Peace

is something I could imagine
in my younger days
sitting in Quaker silence
with Ami and Rudi
my husband at West Falmouth Meetinghouse
or with Chouteau Chapin
and Oscar Bonney
at Damarascotia Meeting
or even twenty years ago
at Sandpoint Meeting
at the hobbitlike house
the few times
I sat in silent meditation
imagining a better world
but then I left the country

Micronesia a dozen years
I find that hope I once had
something so ephemeral
has evaporated

Bill Kemmett

Between Channels

I'm watching the news over
Baghdad. In the distance percussions
resemble heat-lightning in Florida.
CNN news is stationed in a building
across from a mosque. A man is talking
in low tones, as if reporting
a golf tournament.

The beginning of the end is becoming
routine. My wife is making tea
in the kitchen. I turn off the TV.
How was the game, she wants to know.
The Patriots are losing, I said.

We go to bed. She is reading
a novel. I open a National Geographic,
circa 1985 and look at photos
of what could be the city of Ur.
The earliest forms of writing are
engraved on shards of clay tablets
where civilization it is said, began.

GLORIA MINDOCK

When I was younger, grade school age, I questioned: why do people kill each other? Here I am, older, and about to retire, and I still have the same question. I will never understand all the slaughter. Living is a gift and it is not appreciated by those who take lives. Power, money, greed, racism, ethnic cleansing, and religion seem to be many of the reasons for the killing and a norm in so many countries.

In my writing, I try to be a voice for those who have no voice. This is to bring awareness to those who do not realize how bad it is or to wake up those who turn a blind eye to it. Turning a blind eye is what much of the world is good at. Sad, isn't it?

Carrying the Branch is an important anthology. It is an honor to be a part of it. Here we are in this huge world trying to make a difference promoting peace. I will never give up hope that peace will happen. It starts with one hand reaching for another.

I am very fortunate to be born in America where I have freedom to say and do what I want without fear. Many people in some countries do not have this luxury. There is so much hate. Innocent people are caught in the crossfire. Some flee, some don't, and some die trying.

Can you imagine a world at peace sharing resources and helping one another? We must break the chain of hell. The hell is spreading and we can stop it. I do believe in love, kindness, caring, and helping. I have been a social worker/ counselor for most of my life.

Change starts in your heart with everything that you do, say and how you act. All we can do is be a power of example and never give up striving for peace.

Flavia Cosma

Peace

I was explored by a new peace
And I smelled of the earth of flowers, of rain—
Space danced with a doe's feet,
Slim, sensual;
I took in the world as light.

A new understanding,
Perhaps known earlier,
Forgotten once—
I recognized your name
Without shaking the gates of sleep.
Beyond the senseless verge of memory,
I rested between seasons,
Smiled.

Flavia Cosma

The First Day of the Year

The first day of the year was
Wrapped up in peace,
Endless peace, flowing from the sky.

We paused on the road
To look at our footprints
Abandoned on the soft blanket,
And to reflect upon our passage on earth,
While slowly
Our traces disappeared
Under white, innocent snow.

Flavia Cosma

The Season of Love

Calm light
Early in the morning
Gently melts
The shadows of the night.

Objects, grey and blue forms,
Are jolted from sleep;
Substance returns to itself;
Daily life rises from the waves.

Imperfection recedes, yields;
Awed, we find ourselves again,
Complete and beautiful,
Filled with grace.

Peace surround us
With a grandmother's wings.
We reflect tenderly
On our fiercest enemies.
With willowy arms
We want to smooth their wrinkled, rough brows
And gather the tired, shortened flight
Into silky, silvery laps
Of the pious mornings
Of the young winter.

Susan Lewis

Trojan

First we built the horse. Then we had to decide who it was for. The options were legion. Viewed from the proper point of view, everyone was an enemy. We were compelled to build more horses. Secrecy was a problem, until later, when we wanted them to know what we could do. Then there was the challenge of simultaneous deployment. A festival of gift-giving! We named the day something grandiose, then boom! There we were, without enemies. What we did have was one last horse. On Independence Day we wheeled it in.

Susan Lewis

Inheritance

In the beginning, there was hot & odorous gas. Then, certain molecules met & bonded. Their offspring began a long tradition of surpassing their progenitors, before whom they pridefully strutted their new bells & whistles. In no time, gas gave rise to leaf, leaf gave rise to scale, scale gave rise to fur, until the spoiled & doted-upon baby of the family couldn't resist wrecking his inheritance.

Susan Lewis

Our Turn (A Summary)

In the beginning, there was damp & grit & the sucking of bones. Then, there were treasures to kill & die for. Eventually, the treasures were so huge they required the backs of entire continents to support them. Finally, those backs buckled, & it was someone else's turn.

Susan Lewis

Another War
(text for musical setting by Jonathan Golove)

While the odd horse
whinnies itself some stripes.

In some circumstances,
we prefer surrender.

Breathing,
like wine in a cask.

Tick.

Clouds soak neglect
while children wait

for the next sorrow.
Like a bird

chasing diamonds,
mindlessly determined.

Tick.

Missiles, and other
modern messages.

Flow of water on skin,
softening like chocolate.

Claws, scales,
velcro, glass.

Tick.

Pulse racing at
the thought of impact.

Scent of
trampled thyme.

Scent of bodies
bloating in the sun.

Tick.

Stories swallowed
by the desiccated soil.

Scent of empires
bloating in the sun,

trying to dodge
their own collapse.

Susan Lewis

Spoil

(in memory of Abu Ghraib)

In the photo
      one is blindfolded,
another blind.
      Yet another watches,

fashioning this trophy.
      The hooded figure inert,
draped memorial to himself—
      features removed,

denied the honor
      of antlers on a plaque.
You can learn
      from photos

how to tear
      the body from
the man.
      First take his clothes.

With them, his dignity.
      Stack the bodies
like logs.
      Leash them.

Make them crawl.
       Enlist them in
abomination.
       It helps to laugh,

or ignore the sight
       as if it were
less interesting than
       an empty desk.

Smile for
       the camera if
your better self
       has fled.

You don't need a hood
       when your face is
masked, your decency
       severed.

Susan Lewis

The Spirit is Willing

The spirit is willing
but the flesh is

> *(too old)*
> *(too young)*

(lost in these shadows)
(lost in this flickering lie)

while the smoke rising around us
knows no mirror—

unless there is
a second chance

to feel some kind of pleasure
or anything but this stealthy slide—

> *(song of shadows)*
> *(song of light)*

the urge to find the known
despite those sounds seeping under cracks

like breath or tears laced
with vinegar & semen

noble rot &
may I offer

a personal selection
of blessings?

Botrytis or mycelium,
muon or Epoisses?

(tacking on
another even keel)

(here is where you find your eyes)
(here is where you close them)

(here is where you
dream of something more)

water lashed by matter
dark as any doubt,

Solomon splitting
the indivisible

until victory
spoils the prize

for a soldier, say
finally home to

live the ruined rest
after his blood feeds

the fury of the
parched & cratered fields—

Susan Lewis

Amounting To

the type of lure
sought & believed

the plush of fur
bought & received

the tight gleam of
tooth & claw

with the relation of
cloth to flesh

as in address
as in constriction

as in the same,
not the same

amounting to
a shedding & a trading

an assumption of risk
or authenticity

describing this guise
devising this size

grinding like gravel
kicked & shot

crashed & fraught
amounting to

the slip of bone on bone
as cruel as knowing & not

the fine gleam of plied fur
the frayed hide of flayed cur

water & dust at war
for the fading light

the slight hope
of connection

the bare glance
welcomed

amounting to
men with slack hearts

consuming the
future

Susan Lewis

Owner's Automate

For a thought in your head,
select *maybe*.

For the wind in your hair,
choose *emotion*.

Submerge desire in any cubicle
(immerse hands in spilt milk).

To stimulate ambition,
emulsify despair.

Flex a moral muscle
(or satisfy another's craving).

Optimistic accessories may be
hopelessly adjoined.

Press *pantsuit* (male or female).
Repeat.

Energy void if inhibited.
Sympathy skewed if inherited.

All promises, express or implied,
may be broken by unwarranted assumption.

In the event of nuclear *frisson*
press *escape*.

Susan Lewis

Civilization

waiting for worlds
out of sight

out of bounds
(safe, unsound)

the smell of time
parsing sagely

into more of the unsame
mouth of the insane

singing without
rhyme or reason

tongue tickling
time & season

shadow-boxing any
kind of future

crying *back, back*
sighing *lack, lack*

while the pen scratches
no one's itch

& wrong words
muffle the competition

+ their noisy recognition
(saying something known)

until a bell rings
warning us not to think

*there are killers
in charge*

(can we use the other 90%?)
(& by opposing, end them?)

& the victims add an
ominous silence

Dorothy Shubow Nelson

Korea

Slowly the truths of war revealed

About bodies stacked like cords of wood

On top the frozen earth in winter

30 degrees below zero

Never buried in impenetrable ground

Left behind no names

No healing wall of names

No burial

Left on top a mountain range

Left over the hill

Remaining still in the heart's eyes

Of that warrior looking back.

Dorothy Shubow Nelson

Lucky Riders

No one has to tell us to look
at ducks in the water

or swans that spill into a cove even
in the poorest town.

I saw two women fishing in a deserted spot
taking it seriously.

Further on a man drove a truck with a crusher
flattening barrels and old machines.

I want to spend the rest of my life on a train
crisscrossing the earth till I've erased all thoughts
of Jews on trains heading to their deaths.

I'll see mothers reading stories to their children
feeding them snacks

strangers sitting near each other talking
older folks walking in the aisles

no guards at the stations or in the cars.

Dorothy Shubow Nelson

Still Warm

The afternoon is still warm
not blinding
the crowd has thinned
it's been a day to relive
the pain of centuries
evil has a course to run
until we see (each one)
that categories kill

It takes this long to stop
mocking the turtle
some things were not heard
imagination is revelation
at last you know how long
it lives and how it dies

Join the voices on the underside
let the sun find you
unexpectedly
on your way around
now and then appear
as a large mound
in the sea.

Tim Suermondt

The World Isn't Ending

Every generation has its flashpoints
which lead to conflagrations, where men,
women and children are strewn about—
and sometimes a dog sitting on the rubble

of a house that could have been anyone's.
But the theologian who wrote "we must
remember the world is also meek and kind"
was right, like driving down the Taconic Parkway

and my wife reminding me of people we knew
who lived in the area, including some friends
I had shamelessly almost forgotten—"Wave
to Lee," she said, executing a brisk wave herself

and adding "The world is beautiful" and it was
for the entire drive—forests and deer, a strange
gift shop selling wooden clogs and the owner's dog
curled in a corner, watching everyone with delight.

Tim Suermondt

Remembering the Ones
Who Didn't Come Back

Usually when it rains—
though never of monsoon proportions.

A young woman tramps down
a dirt road with an old ox

whose bell around its neck
can be heard even with a transport

plane roaring overhead. A soldier

holds his rifle with one hand,
and waves to the woman with the other.

She waves back: a touching scene
the world is still capable of.

We keep our umbrellas close by now—
they trained us so well.

Tim Suermondt

Mr. Rojas

He knows a real revolution—
beatings and prisons
instead of late night talks in cafes
and shouts of solidarity from afar.

He spins his stories better
than a spider if it could—any trace
of bitterness in the beginning
forgotten for hope at the end.

He'll suggest "Let's walk a poem"
and recite one he believes he wrote,
often saying "beautiful as a senorita"—
often holding onto my arm for balance.

Pui Ying Wong

At Night When the Air Stirs

The war is in the distance
 but coffins arrive at night by plane
as we sleep in our house and the pipes
 are the only things that weep.

When Salvator Giunta was awarded
 the Medal of Honor he spoke
of his dead buddies and the night
 when the sky had more bullets than stars.

I had marched against the war
 and heard my own voice soar and dip
and slip like a fish back to the sea.

In a city called Hom the dictator's bombs
 drop on his people and a survivor
lashes out at the TV cameras, asking
 why do you watch us die?

In the quiet of my house I look out
 and see neither bullets nor stars
I watch and watch, my tongue tied.

Pui Ying Wong

Photographs in Three Shades

The girl's blond hair flying as she walks with the soldiers who carry no rifles. What is she doing by their side? She's their daughter without the teddy bear. She's the Catholic child dressed for communion. In the background silver birches, and poplars so tall they are out of the frame.

Is the baby finally at rest, rocked in the basket-raft, eyes hollowed out? Drifting downstream with nothing between him and the sky, as in the time when he was born. Born to whom loved by whom, along what river what earth, we'll never know.

Here is the boy soldier in a soccer field. In a lunge position he must have been standing guard forever. Next to him a skeleton slumps, bled-out, grimy like statues in abandoned palaces. To the camera the boy, his eyes glinting like blades, seems to be saying, "He's all mine. Bastard!"

Pui Ying Wong

Sunday: Grand Army Plaza

A clown practices silence,
 a mother with a wailing child
waves off the ice cream vendor,
 an elderly man holds a bouquet
in the bend of his arm
 like a newborn.

After a time when every day
 the sky presses down,
long nights when even the streets
 crackle with grief,
we feast on apples, fresh milk,
 like a patient, ravenous after a long illness.

But on the monuments human action
 dies: spears aim only at midair,
half-raised hooves that go nowhere,
 the general's roar expires on his lips.
And in the folds of remembrance's
 black sheen, nothing but blood and tears.

MELISSA STUDDARD

and when we speak we are afraid
our words will not be heard
nor welcomed
but when we are silent
we are still afraid
so it is better to speak
   —*Audre Lorde*

Now will the poets sing.—
Their cries go thundering
Like blood and tears
Into the nation's ears,
Like lightning dart
Into the nation's heart.
   —*Countee Cullen*

Some may ask "Why poetry? What can poetry offer a world fraught with hierarchical thinking, institutionalized abuses, and imperialistic drives?"

Unlike strictly functional communication, which often flies through and away, poetry arrives pregnant and remains to roost and hatch. Poetic language, nestled deep within the tissue of the body, can disrupt the patterns and unexamined choices that preserve harmful structures and belief systems, lifting the blinders and revealing that which it has been instilled in us to overlook.

Likewise, poetry can implant new ideas about ways of being, thinking, and acting. Through the nuances of imagery and language, connections not readily available to the conscious mind are activated, and we feel the power of the imagination to direct us to new realities. Simmering just beneath the surface of the words are ideas about how we might support people and communities who seem unlike ourselves, or how we might begin dismantling systems responsible for the devaluation of human life and the life of our planet and its creatures. Though we don't even know we are thinking it, ideas about how to engage in peaceful and compassionate conflict resolution have begun to bloom.

I believe it's simply not possible to have the collective, poetically curated and rendered effects of war, violence, and aggression hatch inside you and not grow more attuned to the urgency of the work we must do.

Poetry is not inaction. It is the horse action rides in on. It is the train and tracks and countryside all in one, rolling not past but deeply into us, carrying us when we cannot carry ourselves, to destinations we may not have already fully imagined. Yet, as poetry imagines them for us, so we begin to imagine them ourselves, and so they can become.

Rita Dove

Parsley

1. The Cane Fields

There is a parrot imitating spring
in the palace, its feathers parsley green.
Out of the swamp the cane appears

to haunt us, and we cut it down. El General
searches for a word; he is all the world
there is. Like a parrot imitating spring,

we lie down screaming as rain punches through
and we come up green. We cannot speak an R—
out of the swamp, the cane appears

and then the mountain we call in whispers *Katalina.*
The children gnaw their teeth to arrowheads.
There is a parrot imitating spring.

El General has found his word: *perejil.*
Who says it, lives. He laughs, teeth shining
out of the swamp. The cane appears

in our dreams, lashed by wind and streaming.
And we lie down. For every drop of blood
there is a parrot imitating spring.
Out of the swamp the cane appears.

2. The Palace

The word the general's chosen is parsley.
It is fall, when thoughts turn

to love and death; the general thinks
of his mother, how she died in the fall
and he planted her walking cane at the grave
and it flowered, each spring stolidly forming
four-star blossoms. The general

pulls on his boots, he stomps to
her room in the palace, the one without
curtains, the one with a parrot
in a brass ring. As he paces he wonders
Who can I kill today. And for a moment
the little knot of screams
is still. The parrot, who has traveled

all the way from Australia in an ivory
cage, is, coy as a widow, practising
spring. Ever since the morning
his mother collapsed in the kitchen
while baking skull-shaped candies
for the Day of the Dead, the general
has hated sweets. He orders pastries
brought up for the bird; they arrive

dusted with sugar on a bed of lace.
The knot in his throat starts to twitch;
he sees his boots the first day in battle
splashed with mud and urine
as a soldier falls at his feet amazed—
how stupid he looked!— at the sound
of artillery. *I never thought it would sing*
the soldier said, and died. Now

the general sees the fields of sugar
cane, lashed by rain and streaming.
He sees his mother's smile, the teeth
gnawed to arrowheads. He hears
the Haitians sing without R's
as they swing the great machetes:
Katalina, they sing, *Katalina,*

mi madle, mi amol en muelte. God knows
his mother was no stupid woman; she
could roll an R like a queen. Even
a parrot can roll an R! In the bare room
the bright feathers arch in a parody
of greenery, as the last pale crumbs
disappear under the blackened tongue. Someone

calls out his name in a voice
so like his mother's, a startled tear
splashes the tip of his right boot.
My mother, my love in death.
The general remembers the tiny green sprigs
men of his village wore in their capes
to honor the birth of a son. He will
order many, this time, to be killed

for a single, beautiful word.

Notes:
On October 2, 1937, Rafael Trujillo (1891-1961), dictator of the Dominican Republic,
ordered 20,000 blacks killed because they could not pronounce the letter "r" in perejil, the
Spanish word for parsley.

Kaveh Akbar

Palmyra

after Khaled al-Asaad

bonepole bonepole since you died
there's been dying everywhere
do you see it slivered where you are
between a crown and a tongue the question still
more god or less I am all tangled
in the smoke you left the swampy herbs
the paper crows horror leans in and brings
its own light this life so often inadequately
lit your skin peels away your bones soften
your rich unbecoming a kind of apology

when you were alive your cheekbones
dropped shadows across your jaw I saw a picture
I want to dive into that darkness smell
the rosewater the sand   irreplaceable
jewel how much of the map did you leave
unfinished there were so many spiders
your mouth a moonless system
of caves filling with dust
the dust thickened to tar
your mouth opened and tar spilled out

Ocean Vuong

Untitled (Blue, Green, & Brown): oil on canvas: Mark Rothko: 1952

The TV said the planes have hit the buildings.
& I said Yes because you asked me to stay.
Maybe we pray on our knees because the lord
only listens when we're this close
to the devil. There is so much I want to tell you.
How my greatest accolade was to walk
across the Brooklyn Bridge & not think
of flight. How we live like water: touching
a new tongue with no telling
what we've been through. They say the is sky is blue
but I know it's black seen through too much air.
You will always remember what you were doing
when it hurts the most. There is so much
I want to tell you—but I only earned
one life. & I took nothing. Nothing. Like a pair of teeth
at the end. The TV kept saying The planes...
The planes...& I stood waiting in the room
made from broken mocking birds. Their wings throbbing
into four blurred walls. Only you were there.
You were the window.

Kelli Russell Agodon

Altered Landscape

Because these days, the news
is as wide as the sky,
but we are unsure

if it's blue—which shade
of blue, an alternate shade
of blue, or maybe bluer.

Because we're standing
on the edge of a landscape,
not knowing if it's the right

or best or safe landscape,
we gaze outside the frame
to see white, and no words

can fill up the space.
Because we know the difference
between windblown and dying,

because we trust the beauty
of the world to come through.
We each will see America

as a photograph, ripped
or glossy, black and white
or Kodachrome.

And if we each look closely,
some will see the cannon,
others will see the moon.

Gregory Pardlo

Landscape with Intervention

Sun white as a hambone and rain soon despite. Elbowed
and gibbous, sun squirrels through the leaf-roof in spasms
and spills into the arms of the still laddering casualties
of that arboreal coil toward light and the bark-mangy trunks
fossiled into lesser light and those leaning like ski jumpers atop
the ages of mossy, deckle-edged rock along the hillside wall
      where light collects

down, finally, through dampened lashes and pools
beneath my eyes' tear-tasseled hoods. Here's where I come to sit
and look, hoping to see—apprehend the images of things. And
I'm reminded of the Hopi ban on the camera. How it is a kind of
embargo and copyright, as well as superstition, with reaching
implications regarding easement across shadows, reflections
      held in escrow by spirits of the lake.

What it says about art, its dialogue with the injunction against
representation in the Islamic tradition, hinting at the ethics involved.
For example, I imagine I am the reader of this poem decades from now
and have to wonder in what draft the woman began to appear.
Scaffolding
gone, I could mistake the idea for fact, in the lapse fashion reality
from the merely literal or guild history until it's kitsch. Which is worse:
      The War of the Worlds

snafu or our initial response to Mount Rushmore? Oddly
compelling, both border religion in a quandary of cause
and effect: the flock flows over the cliff as if it were tipped from
a glass, and our estimation of the men cast in stone might grow
in step with our perception of the effort they inspired in Borglum
(though, no less inspiration has the younger artist who simply
      carves his heart's

name in a tree). And is it not said, "The child sees no end
to her suffering and that makes hers more real than our own"?
Belief is itself a cause—of which truth is a corollary effect.
Light-play through the leaves leaves each glance a smear like
the proximate viewed through binoculars. Sunrays frayed
like shoestrings. I like what Rodin told Rilke to do: go
          to the zoo and watch

the animals until you see them. I imagine him on a bench
in the *Jardin des Plantes* thinking and unthinking *Panther, Panther,*
Panther, Panther. Something larcenous in this as well unless
there breeds sympathy in the friction (fiction?) between sight and
what's seen, the way kids often bond when they brawl. Some of my
students in the Bronx transliterate their graffiti tags from the names
          of automobiles and boast

having carved them on windows of subway trains: Cherokee,
Navigator, Sequoia. They laugh now when I use these names
in class. The sky features boiled milk shot through with bleeds
of black ink spreading like Novocain, solving for gray over
variants of eggshell and roseate bone. Arpeggio of geese.
A chopper makes a slipper pivot like a mouse on waxed
          linoleum, chivvying the treetops

on the hill beside condos. In the clearing below the access
road, flags pop like Ps in a microphone and no one else in sight
sees the dishwasher toking in the car out back of the caterer's,
dishrag on his shoulder like a tiny epaulette, his windshield gone
white with mist. For years he must have taken these Pennsylvania
roads with paranoiac care, rubber-necking at the yoga of chassis
          beneath wrinkled sheets

of metal, fiberglass chafed and chipped, quarter panels warped
like vinyl records in the sun. I wonder if censorship does protect us
like seat belts in the caroming coach of contagion, the power
of suggestion polluting the air like tailpipe emissions? I'd a friend
who'd decline to give his name without acquaintance first, fearing
chants and mantras formed from his appellative
          turf conjuring away

186

his essence like some bootleg golem. A minor soap actor, he'd
complain about viewers condemning him for his character's
behavior on the show. He once told me his craft was frowned on
in England before the Restoration as it was felt vice attended such
impractical use of creativity. Accordingly, among actors, fathers
encouraged the mingling of identity and act by raising
           their sons in dedication

to a single role—the way craftsmen took their trade to be
their name: carpenter, tailor, the ubiquitous
smith—and stack eternal odds in their favor: that the Calvinist
god's estimation of the man match the quality of that man's
performance in the role he'd been given. Such piety doubling
as social currency, suggesting an audience of more than
           just one. The American

actor, Thomas Dartmouth Rice, developed a role in the late
1820's which he dedicated his life to performing. He covered
his white face in burnt cork and dubbed himself "Jim Crow".
His influence was epidemic. Drunk driving heaps like
public art bound for parade grounds of local high schools
surfed throaty flatbeds, interiors denuded by jaws
           of life, lifeless and bereft

of sex appeal as driver's ed. props while, I envision,
our dishman gawked at police shucking shards and paint
samples from trees' puckered trunks as totems against loss
of property, watched police depict angles of impact on
clipboards like carvings in reverence of chance, like the
converging logics of property, religion and art.
           Late one evening,

let's say having discovered the wreck while driving home,
he felt obliged to stay on hand. Like one sitting through
the credits, he stayed through the scuttlebutt, saw cops cup
matches like the ingrown stems of imaginary fruit, fire at the
core kindling their cigs, those paper snorkels growing
dark with drops sieved through the umbrage
           above. The area

pockmarked with the pink soot and spent shells of road flares.
But hasn't it all just happened, if saying it makes it so? "Let there
be light...," "These are not your droids...," etcetera, etcetera?
I'll try this one: "There is no interest on my student loans." Or,
"This Metro Card is not expired." How I wish art were as
magical as corporate accounting and I could reverse this sequence,
      undo its corollary and coalesce

flames back into dusty matchsticks like magician's bouquets
gasped into the wand, retract the 10-45 form police dispatch
and subsequent requests for EMS, relieve the dishman of his
eventual discovery at shift's end, stuff clouds of combustion
into the manifold like unfolded clothes into a suitcase
and bungee the woman now sitting like Wyeth's Christina,
      sobbing on the roadside berm,

back into the open top of her just-wrecked cabriolet. There's
still candle wax and a dirty wreath by the adjacent tree
from moths ago after some classmate's kegger. But like
the man says about his painting, *"Ceci n'est pas une pipe."*
No one need be convinced. Any of this beyond the glow
of the laptop, the hum of the AC through the ducts. Any of this
      beyond nostalgia and the ground-

hog in the yard unaware of its own mortality, the road raveling by.
Herewith, I proclaim the orthodoxies intended to preclude our kind
of prodigality are disinherited. Our convergence is inevitable, my
Galatea, heretic reader, Gregory. You have my eyes, though my face
slipped from your craggy face long ago. See through me, the
illusion of orthodoxy. And you, admit it, are conspiring in these
      impractical, aesthetic

diversions, in my misgivings about the surety of retirement plans
and of eternal souls. Enjoy this small thing with me, it's no
bother. Let us doubt together. If the Promised Land and the
Mountaintop exceed your expectations, will you wonder, Greg—
if I may, will you wonder, on arrival, Greg, if you really were
so godless as to let that woman lay there, unaided
      for all this world to see?

Joan Naviyuk Kane

Nunaqtigiit
(people related through common possession of territory)

The enemy misled that missed the island in the fog,
I believe in one or the other, but both exist now
   to confuse me. Dark from dark.

Snow from snow. I believe in one—

Craggy boundary, knife blade at the throat's slight swell.

From time to time the sound of voices
   as through sun-singed grass,

or grasses that we used to insulate the walls of our winter houses—
walrus hides lashed together with rawhide cords.

So warm within the willows ingathered forced into leaf.

I am named for your sister Naviyuk: call me apo⊠.

Surely there are ghosts here, my children sprung
   from these deeper furrows.

The sky of my mind against which self-
   betrayal in its sudden burn
   fails to describe the world.

We, who denied the landscape
   and saw the light of it.

Leaning against the stone wall ragged
I began to accept my past and, as I accepted it,

I felt, and I didn't understand:
   I am bound to everyone.

Amy King

Perspective

When I see the two cops laughing
after one of them gets shot
because this is TV and one says
while putting pressure on the wound,
Haha, you're going to be fine,
and the other says, *I know, haha!,*
as the ambulance arrives—
I know the men are white.
I think of a clip from the hours
of amateur footage I've seen
when another man at an intersection
gets shot, falls, and bleeds from a hole
the viewer knows exists only by the way
the dark red pools by the standing cop's feet,
gun now holstered, who
yells the audience back to the sidewalk.
I know which one is dying
while black and which one stands by white.
I think this morning about the student
in my class who wrote a free write line
on the video I played
that showed a man pouring water
on his own chest, "...the homoerotic
scene against a white sky" with no other men
present. *Who gets to see and who follows
what script?* I ask my students.
Whose lines are these and by what hand
are they written?

Kazim Ali

Mosque in Gallilee

—to Rachel Tzvia Back

Sketching the outlines of the country
I know by heart now how far I travel
From Haifa to the eastern sea
Listening to how long history echoes

We passed a ruined mosque on the road
Not knowing if it was destroyed in 48 or 67 or 73
One side of the room lying open to the fields
Inside the walls marked by graffiti in four languages

The mihrab blackened by fire
Not less holy and still marking direction
Across the street a dead cow lying on its side
Three ropes hang down from the minaret

Some Hasidic boys have scaled up the side
And sit on the balcony eating sandwiches
Or were they saying their prayers.
Perhaps they were listening to the language of the land,

Or the abandoned mosque, or the limp carcass
On the side of the road?

Kazim Ali

Bil'in

"From our roof you can see Tel Aviv, and then the sea."

The evening in the distance speaks the tongue of fire

Empty canisters glitter in the field

The light shines always in the next country but in our country
Darkness has no ration limit

We translate the Hill of Spring in our language of snow

Night lies down here on our roof in August

Listen to the sound of the fountains on the other side of the wall

A long time before we had any argument about historiography
each woman here grew wild thyme in the bullet-laden garden

Each man measured in his mind the distance between his jail cell
and the eastern shore of the sea

Pamela Uschuk

Ode to Federico Garcia Lorca

Federico, sometimes you come to me as a little rain
straining up from the south, smeared
with the scent of orange rind and blood.
Smeared with rabbit blood frenzy, coyotes
ring the house howling the hour
the moon ticks like a gypsy watch
above the pool where the heron sleeps.
Where the heron dreams, a smear
the size of the moon is actually a guitar
moaning the syllables of your lost name.
Federico, when you come to me, the unbearable
longing of trees roots deeper in the sky, flies
among stars like a comet in search
of its dead twin. Federico the wind tonight is arctic
silver, not green, not forever green,
and I think how easy it is to die, skin basted
with orange blossoms and loneliness
as if loneliness was a horse a poet could break
or deny. Tonight, you are the slivered silver moon
ticking above cedar and sage that remember
their roots in the olive groves of Andalusia.
Green rind of death, how dare you spit
out the syllables of such desire? Federico,
some nights you fly through the window,
the eye of a hawk on fire,
black gaze gone to blood, gone
to the ropey bones of moonlight,
to guitars laughing in blue pines,
to the wet bulls of passion,
to the weft of love abandoned
to oiled rifles in an olive grove
on a sunny day before I was born. Did
they so fear the delicacy of your hands?

Pamela Uschuk

I Have an Illegal Alien In My Trunk

Just north of the border, *la migra* doesn't consider
this bumper sticker a joke. Only a Chihuahua without papers,
maybe a pair of pawned cowboy boots
would fit in the trunk of this mini SUV driving Oracle
swarming at rush hour. Even though half of Tucson's traffic
speaks Spanish, the legislature's declared
English the only legal fuel—
it's the same Continental Divide stubborn and paralytic
as the steel-plated wall insulting our nation's learning curve
as it cleaves us.

For over seventy years
my grandma's high cheekbones were illegal. Lovely
as a tiger lily she spoke
the six severed tongues dividing her heart.
In a grave that does not spell out her name
in any language, she is beyond the shovels of police
who would have to dig up her bones to deport them
back to a village outside Prague, where
beneath a Catholic church are layered
the crumbling skulls and femurs
of her ancestors slaughtered by Black Plague
and centuries of wars.

I am safe for now in my adobe house
with its rainbow congregation of chuckling quails,
pyrrhuloxia, choirs of mockingbirds,
skitterish purple finches, coyotes,
javelinas, rattlers, scorpions, leopard lizards,
and the not so silent majority of English sparrows
who accommodate too easily to walls—there
is not one passport among them.

The cactus wren weaves her tough nest
among the barbed thorns of the cholla, while
round-eared gophers construct
complex subways for their babies to run
under chain link fences separating yards.

Each day along the border of our sealed hearts
gleaming with coiled razor wire, traffic
idles waiting for armed guards
to pillage each car trunk for contraband
people and drugs. I have seen our agents rip
out the interiors of vans, spit commands
at old women with black hair and dark skin.
Sanitary, they use rubber gloves
to deconstruct the grocery bags
and plastic purses of common lives.
Indians are particularly suspect, even though
reservations were drawn like tumors by both governments
to spill across borders, so that whole families
are amputated like unnecessary limbs.

This morning walking the Rillito River,
we read bilingual signs warning the thirsty
not to drink irrigation water ringing ornamental bushes
& flowering trees. This year, statistics say,
twice as many border crossers will die of thirst
in Arizona. Who can stop tongues
alien or otherwise from swelling black at noon. After all,
in the barbed wire waiting room of the heart
there is no seating for sentiment
nor room for the frail arms of hope to save strangers, even
if they are nursing mothers or desperate fathers
looking for work who haven't yet learned
the English word for *por que.*
After all, waging a war on terror
like any war is not for the faint ambitions of the humane, so
in the game of homeland security,
we erect a bulletproof wall across the borders of our souls
that guarantees destruction must win.

Saba Syed Razvi

Of Birds, Of Prey

If you were eight years old, awake
early enough in the morning for the treat of a walk
with your older brothers, worldwise and unweary yet,
you might feel big in your trousers,
chappals, big enough to see the wonders of the sky.

If you were eight years old then, and roaring,
like lions, like tigers, two planes emerged
from the poles of the horizon, erupting
into a dogfight over your own veranda,
you might think it was a game. Such a show of. Until
the horror on your brothers' faces showed otherwise.

And if you were eight years old still,
heart racing in the center of a circle
of siblings, your father and same brothers armed
heavier than the servants, you might have stayed
up all night, tense as a violin string
because the communists were coming over the fields,
because your father was appointed
by the British and India discovered an urge for freedom.

And what if you were still eight, traveling in a coal car,
a formation of aeroplanes like geese flying overhead?
Covered with soot and holding breath, you might begin
to understand how the world bears cruelty in the horizon's arms —
it's certainty in the metal birds
that freedom for Hyderabad had been lost. At any moment
the train could screech to a halt, armed men checking
each boxcar.

If you were eight years old, the war raging all around you and
only just over the horizon, you would not feel the way forward
was a promise. You would know better
than to resort to the contentious names for things, the names
everyone wants to choose – an apple is the fruit that made you fall
in love with the world, a cloud of smoke is a reminder of hearth
and home, needing the wanderer's safe return. A man is nothing
but a body made of clay, made of longing and fear, in need of a name.

If you were eight years old when fighter planes roared
beyond your head, you would wonder at the way fire had gone
from hearth to heart of artillery, and you might wonder what words
and what beyond words keeps safe the questioning glance, and you
would remember that beyond the gates of your door was nothing
sure as death. Atmosphere carrying the threat of ambush:
not every dancer is a dervish;
what is the difference between a dogfight and a drone?

At seventy-eight, you would have never forgotten the taste of fear,
coal in your lungs, silence. Your world-curious, word-wise daughters – never
safe. How can you explain it to them, the danger of a voice, a perfect sky,
how quickly a stroll can pull you under the rain
of revolution? Any sky can burst in a moment. Any man – a hunter,
turning weak before a tiger.

Saba Syed Razvi

Nightmare of Ritual and Release

In the language of our shared heritage, the number three,
the number three,
the number three bears a ritual significance.

In the language of our shared heritage,
the gates of paradise rest at the feet of the mother,
the woman who bears us, who bears...all of us, and all besides.

Because, you say, the world of the creator belongs to those who believe.
Because you always believed that for those who believed in their God,
the letting go of this life is a release.

In the language of our shared heritage,
death is only a return to the embrace of the creator, womb of the eternal mother,
for those who are steadfast in faith and belief.

But, for those who hesitate, pacing back and forth, back and forth, back and –
is it forth if you refuse to go forward, if you live in the past like it never changed ? –

forth? The door opens and closes on reality and I walk
into the room and out of the room and avoid the third time.

In the language of our shared heritage, the number three means consent,
means a certain acknowledgment,

means I cannot bite my tongue again to taste the red of our shared heritage
to avoid walking into a room bearing you but not you.

As I think of you, I think of you, thinking of your own mother.
As I think of you, I think of your own grief.
As I think of you, I cannot bear to walk into that room and bear the weight of my grief.

It is the ritual washing of the body that I remember. You taught me this, myself, my sister,
my other sister, three. You taught me this. And without you, I have lost them, too. The red
of my bitten lip, the cells that will tell me what came before what will come again.

The mother, the maiden, the crone.
The lover, the liver, the stone.
The mother, my mother, my own.

I raise your hand, chant a prayer, chant a prayer, right first and rinse the water thrice over each.
Your gold bracelets not chiming like bells, your fingers broad like mine, your nails, strong like
mine, you said I had your hands; so, I think of your hands washing mine.

I raise your left hand thrice beneath the water, watch the water fall downward
through the drain in the floor, watch the water slip down the drain, as when you
bathed the body of your own mother, that water took with it the band of your wedding ring.

I wash your face, face like my own face, face that I cannot face
Because as long as I have wanted you to understand my voice or my own words,
I cannot see you face me, now, voice the words, now, that I would hear, now.

Before I wrap your body in a sheet,
before I let you go from me,
before I recognize what you say that death for the beloved of God is a relief,

I wash your arms. I wash your feet. First the right three times, then the left three times,
With you my heritage ends, with me, your lineage ends; such time until we meet again.
Paradise lies under the feet of the mother, Paradise rests beneath the feet of the mother.

Saba Syed Razvi

Beside the Muezzin's Call and the Harem's Veil: the Ordinary Adam, this Eve.

Beyond the call of the tearful muezzin ringing from minarets and medieval days, beyond the veil of the harems' unwalled pillars, its courtyard of courtesans and curves, fountains wet with oases of longing, for the parched past mirage, the world of the unwanted Arab Spring beckons, the world past the colony and the empire, past the purpled, puckered, promise of an ancient echo of a renascence long past. Beside the bragging rights of the terrorist and the terrified, the vilified and victimized, the silence of the voiceless echoes, the call to prayer and to arms, to hearth and to home and to harbor, the *zagreet* and the wail and the worried echo, beseeching or seeking, the sound of the shudder under the warplane's war cry. Beyond this, beside this, waiting for the storm to pass lies the ordinary man, the Adam with hurts as commonplace as blue jeans, his skin as alien as some ancient blue. The ordinary woman with an ordinary womb, and the curves and cries of Eve. The old man and the thin man. The seductress and the dance of her seven veils. The borrowed promise of a people to weigh the scales of some man's fat greed. And all the blameless believers, believing in nothing but a hope beyond the word beside the man who judges what is ours and what is other. The guileless stand, preemptively judged. Not that sky, but this sky. Not that name, but this name. And every atmosphere from one horizon to another ringing with the thunderous burst of the weight of atom and atom and atom.

Yehuda Amichai

The Diameter of the Bomb
Translated by Chana Bloch

The diameter of the bomb was thirty centimeters
and the diameter of its effective range about seven meters,
with four dead and eleven wounded.
And around these, in a larger circle
of pain and time, two hospitals are scattered
and one graveyard. But the young woman
who was buried in the city she came from,
at a distance of more than a hundred kilometers,
enlarges the circle considerably,
and the solitary man mourning her death
at the distant shores of a country far across the sea
includes the entire world in the circle.
And I won't even mention the howl of orphans
that reaches up to the throne of God and
beyond, making
a circle with no end and no God.

Jenn Givhan

Volver (Bride Price)
for Rahila Muska

I wanted to return the scent of late-
summer, avocados blackening on the branches
on the grass.

All that I love tonight—
the azure monarch laboring toward milkweed,
our lungs expanding in the rains

after running hills at sunset,
canary-yellow of the eggs we'll fry come morning—
might be lost in the morning

if you look at the beauty of the world—
the teenage Afghan poet, girl who named herself
after a smile & called the only radio frequency

      for women, for poetry, for a way out,
girl whose brothers beat her for disgracing them with poems,
with free will, girl who burned

      herself in protest & sang her final poem
from the hospital, & sang her final poem

on the radio, & sang, before she died

I call. You're stone.
One day you'll look & find I'm gone—

but if you look at the ugliness of the world
(all that I love tonight, tonight might be lost)

      you may find a kind of burning.

Jenn Givhan

Protection Spell (Riot's Eye)

They're chasing my boy, his
dreadlocks streaming

behind him like bed sheets
from the second story

window of a house fire.

           He & the asphalt
dovetail

I watch & I watch
like a black hole swallowing

a baby universe. (This is the last
of the gunmetal dreams.)

I wring the blood
from my ribcage

my world in your chest, child.

          When I was a child
I believed God held us

like a paper bag
to the mouth of a panic attack.

         How I'm holding
a city like my boy,

my boy to my own
siren wail—

How the wind-as-breath
                    moved us, bent our

tallest trees
to snapping, like our songs

on our knees.

Jenn Givhan

Warn the Young Ones

First war. We burnish the spine of our own
flesh. Tethered nerve, strangling cord. We

burial mound. We ritual. We
corn stalks in rustling fields. Nothing tribe

nothing sex. Rock for riverbed. Notched
with flint. Second war. We need less. Sequoia

burns. Cities. In our bodies, wrappings
of bodies. One debates running. One debates peeling

skin. One stops debating, begins praying without
knees. Not *for* rain. *Prays* rain. Holy nothing

unlaces nothing remembered nothing
forgiven— Come others. Third war.

I am a void in the particle machine. I am dust.
Fourth war we lose the need for water. We lose

all taste. Rain brings each earthwormed corpse. Nothing
ugly. Turn not. Our faces from the dead. We

resurgence. We fable of bee boxes
& honey. We ark of some lost Kingdom

Animalia. We zebra. We aardvark.
We dredge the flooded streets of us, the gutters.

Fifth war. We grow stronger. All that can be
taken we take. All that can be eaten

we swallow. All that can be broken we
pull into our bellies & release. Nothing is whole.

Sixth war. We lose our appetites. Our bones brittle.
The cabbage in the broth bitters. One suggests

pulling from ribcages. Hearts. Using them
as weapons. Seventh war. The cord we began with.

Nothing like a noose. We would rest. Long for nothing
but rest. Each threaded backbone slips its knot. Nothing

transforms. I want to tell you this is the end. I want.

Ross Gay

A Small Needful Fact

Is that Eric Garner worked
for some time for the Parks and Rec.
Horticultural Department, which means,
perhaps, that with his very large hands,
perhaps, in all likelihood,
he put gently into the earth
some plants which, most likely,
some of them, in all likelihood,
continue to grow, continue
to do what such plants do, like house
and feed small and necessary creatures,
like being pleasant to touch and smell,
like converting sunlight
into food, like making it easier
for us to breathe.

Dave Parsons

Austin Fire

Memories from the day of the University of Texas Tower shootings
& the 100th anniversary of Scholz's Beer Garden on August 1, 1966.

Out of the cave
of European History class
I am struck
by squinting bright skies
strolling on the edge of the shadow
of the university tower shade
through the southeast campus quad
flip flopping to my Mustang
for my short drive to work
less than an hour before
student victim #1
will have fallen
in that very path.

I am traveling back now—
back to the pool—
down the hot tar entry
down the pebbled walkway
to Barton Springs
churning shadowy deep blue—
it's the blues—the gushing
blues 68 degrees year-round
offering a deadening numbness
making the youngest of skin
cadaver cold and this ordinary
workday, I am just another Life-
guard cut loose too soon.

And now—again
I am driving back
again back and away
away from the many
oblique precipices—falls
hidden undercurrents
jutting stones in the blinds
of the limestone aquifer
traveling back under and through
the towering pecan trees
just a short dash—and now again
Barton Springs Road—
The Rolling Stones—Can't Get No
Satisfaction....everything
is heating up the day.

At Scholz's Garden
another grand spring
100 years of beer flowing
unjudgmentally through
the many unruly seasons
through the untold
joyous and unfettered
the anonymous generations
of the deemed and the damned
and all their wagging
Did you know(s)...flying
around the ever blank
pages of air—air that receives, never
recording a single loving or gnashing word
of the produce of this imperfect garden
those sweaty hound dog days—I feel
that very air here again now—the gamey
smells of the Dutchman's beer garden
the care free summer women
laughing braless in loose tie-dyes
swilling nickel Lone Stars
aiming flirtatious glances

then firing their deadly frank stares
swinging suntanned legs
to the juke box beats
Hey, Mr. Tambourine Man
play a song for me...all
positioned between
the two towers: the capital dome
topped with Lady Liberty
and UT's apex and bastille of education
and there now...and again—white puffs—

Sniper! Sniper!

Girls first! diving under
stone gray concrete tables
towering turquoise sky
ragged clouds
ripping the battle blue
drifting...mist like...hiding
momentarily gun site portals,
and our shade tree bunkers
fiery memories
imbedded
like so many stray shots—

He was a crew cut
every mother's son
Boy Scout—Marine
sharpshooter
again all paths of mine—
In his last note to the world
Charles Whitman
requested an autopsy
with special consideration
to his brain...they found
a tiny, cloudy gray mass
of malignant tissue lined
in crimson—seems it's
always the smallest of embers.

William Pitt Root

There is a Permanence
That Obliterates the Present

In that moment required to transfer
lives in a glance,
the light that passes between eyes
has rerouted my life time after time

and I have known
in a manner no court of facts would admit
the fine wrist or steady eye of one
I love in a time parallel to this

or the blue lips of a man
in whose arms I have died
or the broad hands I have killed
or shared bread with on a road

lined with olive trees
as cicadas buzz from the dry shade of stones.
Or I look at a woman and know her
as a father knows the daughter

grieving her lost child,
or as the child has known her,
nuzzling her breast and looking up,
eyes half closed, at the bright chin.

A glance, a tremor in a voice,
the posture a hand assumes
as someone speaks to a stranger,
or simply a human odor

and for an instant this life
is unrecognizable to me
while a code I can neither break nor deny
registers and I respond

with a poem I gaze into later
as into a fire obliterating
the present with its permanence,
hearing as one hears in a shell

the sea suddenly more substantial
than those waves at your ankles
whose foam you may wipe away with that towel
which will never touch the roaring deep within.

William Pitt Root

The Names of the Dead are Being Withheld Pending Notification

What if he's right and these blades of grass are thrust up
from the mouths of the dead
who kept their silence an hour too long?

Every one of us knows what could have been said.
Let's think about it, let's consider it now
while our mouths can still form their miracles

and at the edge of Earth's darkness
that constant green conspiracy gives off
mute sighs of oxygen to sustain our common tongue.

Publication Credits

Kaveh Akbar: "Palmyra" was first published in *The Offing*.

Kazim Ali: "Mosque in Gallilee" and "Bil'in" were first published in *Taos Journal of International Poetry & Art*.

Yehuda Amichai: "The Diameter of the Bomb" in *The Selected Poetry of Yehuda Amichai*, by Yehuda Amichai, edited and translated by Chana Bloch and Stephen Mitchell © 1986 and 1996 Chana Bloch and Stephen Mitchell. Published by the University of California Press.

Margo Berdeshevsky: "Beyond My Used-up Words" first appeared in her book, *Before the Drought* (Glass Lyre Press September 2017.) Published with permission.

W. E. Butts: "Primary" from *Last Poems 2015*, Adastra Press

Lynn Cohen: "Paris" was first published in *Dreams and Dreamers* (2010 Blue Light Press).

Rita Dove: "Parsley" appeared in *Museum* (Pittsburgh: Carnegie Mellon University Press, 1983). Copyright © 1983 by Rita Dove. Reprinted with the permission of the author.

Stewart Florsheim: "The Best Bread in Montparnasse" appeared in The *Short Fall From Grace* (Blue Light Press, 2006). Copyright © by Stewart Florsheim. Reprinted with the permission of the author.

Diane Frank: "A View from the Moon" was first published in *Swan Light* (Blue Light Press).

Ross Gay: "A Small Needful Fact" was first published as poem of the week at *Split This Rock*.

William Pitt Root: "There Is A Permanence That Obliterates The Present" first appeared in *Pamphlet #7*, Mesilla Press. "The Names of the Dead are Being Withheld Pending Notification" originally appeared in *Reasons for Going It on Foot*, Atheneum.

Mary Kay Rummel: "Remembering Paris" from *Cypher Garden*, Blue Light Press, 2017.

Tim Suermondt: "The World Isn't Ending" was first published in *These Fragile Lilacs Journal*. "Remembering the Ones Who Didn't Come Back" was first published in *Taos Journal of Poetry and Art*. "Mr. Rojas" was first published in *The Galway Review* (Ireland).

Lynne Thompson: "Raffia" appeared in *Beg No Pardon* (Perugia Press, 2007). Reprinted with the permission of the author.

Pamela Uschuk: "I Have an Illegal Alien in my Trunk" first appeared in terrain.org. "I Have an Illegal Alien in my Trunk" and "Ode to Federico Garica Lorca" appeared in *Wild in the Plaza of Memory*, Wings Press, 2012.

Ocean Vuong: "Untitled (Blue, Green, & Brown): oil on canvas: Mark Rothko: 1952" was first published in *TriQuarterly*.

Loretta Diane Walker: "Silenced" was first published in The Poetry Society of Texas Book of the Year Prize Poems. "50 Boulevard Voltaire" appeared in *Desert Light* (Beaumont: Lamar University Press, 2017). Copyright © 2017 by Loretta Diane Walker. Reprinted with the permission of the author.

Pui Ying Wong: "At Night When the Air Stirs" was first published in *Foundling Review*. "Sunday: Grand Army Plaza" was first published in *The Southampton Review*.

Contributor Notes

Kelli Russell Agodon is a poet, writer, and editor from the Pacific Northwest. She is the author of six books, most recently, *Hourglass Museum* (Finalist for the Washington State Book Prize and shortlisted for the Julie Suk Prize honoring poetry books from independent presses), *The Daily Poet: Day-By-Day Prompts For Your Writing Practice* (which she co-wrote with Martha Silano), and *Letters from the Emily Dickinson Room*, winner of ForeWord Magazine's Book of the Year in Poetry. Kelli is the cofounder of Two Sylvias Press where she works as an editor and book cover designer. Her work has appeared in magazines such as *The Atlantic, New England Review, The Harvard Review,* and *O, The Oprah Magazine.* www.agodon.com / www.twosylviaspress.com

Kaveh Akbar is the founder and editor of Divedapper, a home for interviews with the most vital voices in contemporary poetry. His poems have appeared in *Poetry, American Poetry Review, Georgia Review, PBS NewsHour, Boston Review,* and elsewhere. Alice James Books will publish his debut full-length collection, *Calling a Wolf a Wolf,* in Fall 2017 and Sibling Rivalry Press will publish his chapbook, *Portrait of the Alcoholic,* in January 2017. Akbar is the recipient of a 2016 Ruth Lilly and Dorothy Sargent Rosenberg Fellowship from the Poetry Foundation and the Lucille Medwick Memorial Award from the Poetry Society of America. He was born in Tehran, Iran and currently lives and teaches in Florida.

Kazim Ali's poetry collections include *Sky Ward* (Wesleyan University Press, 2013),winner of the Ohioana Book Award in Poetry, *The Far Mosque,* winner of Alice James Books' New England/New York Award, *The Fortieth Day* (BOA Editions, 2008), and the cross-genre text *Bright Felon: Autobiography and Cities* (Wesleyan University Press, 2009). He has also published translations of *Water's Footfall* by Sohrab Sepehri (Omnidawn Press, 2011), *Oasis of Now: Selected Poems* by Sohrab Sepehri (BOA Editions, 2013), and (with Libby Murphy) *L'amour by Marguerite Duras* (Open Letter Books, 2013). His novels include *Quinn's Passage* (blazeVox books), named one of "The Best Books of 2005" by *Chronogram* magazine and *The Disappearance of Seth* (Etruscan Press, 2009). His books of essays include *Orange Alert: Essays on Poetry, Art and the Architecture of Silence* (University of Michigan Press, 2010), and *Fasting for Ramadan* (Tupelo Press, 2011). In addition to co-editing *Jean Valentine: This-World Company* (University of Michigan Press, 2012), Ali is a contributing editor for *AWP Writers Chronicle,* associate editor of the literary magazine *FIELD,* and founding editor of the small press Nightboat Books. As well, he is the series co-editor for both *Poets on Poetry* and *Under Discussion,* from the University of Michigan Press. He is an associate professor of Creative Writing and Comparative Literature at Oberlin College.

Tareq Al Jabr is a poet and translator and has published poetry in Syrian, Iraqi and Danish journals. He is a graduate of the University of Damascus.

John Amen is the author of several collections of poetry, including *strange theater* (New York Quarterly Books, 2015), a finalist for the 2016 Brockman-Campbell Award and work from which was chosen as a finalist for the 2016 Dana Award. He is co-author, with Daniel Y. Harris, of *The New Arcana*. His latest collection, *Illusion of an Overwhelm,* was released by New York Quarterly Books in April 2017. His poetry, fiction, reviews, and essays have appeared in journals nationally and internationally, and his poetry has been translated into Spanish, French, Hungarian, Korean, and Hebrew. He founded and continues to edit *The Pedestal Magazine.*

Yehuda Amichai (1924-2000) is widely considered the greatest contemporary Israeli poet, and a pioneering stylist in modern Hebrew.

KB Ballentine's fifth collection, *Almost Everything, Almost Nothing,* was published in 2017 by Middle Creek Publishing. Two collections, *The Perfume of Leaving* and *What Comes of Waiting,* won the 2016 and 2013 Blue Light Press Book Awards. Published in many print and online journals, her work also appears in *River of Earth and Sky: Poems for the Twenty-first Century* (2015), *Southern Poetry Anthology, Volume VI: Tennessee* (2013) and *Southern Light: Twelve Contemporary Southern Poets* (2011). Learn more about KB Ballentine at www.kbballentine.com.

R. Steve Benson was lucky to have studied poetry with the late farmer/poet James Hearst at the University of Northern Iowa. Married with three grown children, Steve is a retired art teacher. He has had 20 poems in the *Christian Science Monitor.* His poems have appeared in many literary journals including the *North American Review, Briar Cliff Review, Weber: The Contemporary West, South Carolina Review, Pirene's Fountain,* and *The Minnesota Review.* He and his brother Barry have published two collections of their poetry: *Schooled Lives — Poems By Two Brothers,* and *Poems By The Skunk River Valley Boys.*'

Margo Berdeshevsky, born in New York city, often writes and lives in Paris. *Before The Drought,* her newest collection, is from Glass Lyre Press, September 2017. (In an early version, it was finalist for the National Poetry Series.) Berdeshevsky is author as well of *Between Soul & Stone,* and *But a Passage in Wilderness,* (Sheep Meadow Press.) Her book of illustrated stories, *Beautiful Soon Enough,* received the first Ronald Sukenick Innovative Fiction Award for Fiction Collective Two (University of Alabama Press.) Other honors include the Robert H. Winner Award from the Poetry Society of America, a portfolio of her poems in the *Aeolian Harp Anthology #1* (Glass Lyre Press,) the *& Now Anthology of the Best of Innovative Writing,* and numerous Pushcart Prize nominations. Her works appear in the American journals: *Poetry International, New Letters, Kenyon Review, Plume, The Collagist, Tupelo Quarterly, Gulf Coast, Southern Humanities Review, Pleiades, Prairie Schooner, The American Journal of Poetry,* & *Jacar Press—One,* among many others. In Europe her works have been seen in *The Poetry Review (UK) The Wolf, Europe, Siècle 21,* & *Confluences Poétiques.* A multi genre novel, *Vagrant,* and a hybrid of poems, *Square Black Key,* wait at the gate. She may be found reading from her books in London, Paris, New York City, or somewhere new in the world. Her *Letters from Paris* may be found in Poetry International, here: http:// pionline.wordpress.com/category/letters-from-paris/ For more info kindly see: http:// margoberdeshevsky.com and http://margoberdeshevsky.blogspot.com

Chana Bloch's many books include *The Song of Songs: A New Translation* and *The Windows: New and Selected Poetry of Dahlia Ravikovitch.*

W.E. Butts (1944-2013) was the author of ten poetry collections, including *Cathedral of Nervous Horses* published in 2012 with Hobblebush Books. *Sunday Evening at the Stardust Café* was winner of the 2006 Iowa Source Poetry Book Prize. His poems appeared in many journals such as *Atlanta Review, Cimarron Review, Mid-American Review, Poetry East,* and elsewhere, and in many anthologies. The recipient of two Pushcart Prize nominations and a Massachusetts Artist Foundation Award, he taught in the BFA in Creative Writing Program at Goddard College. He was the New Hampshire Poet Laureate from 2009 until his death in 2013. His final book of poems, *Story & Luck* was published by Adastra Press in 2015.

Thomas Centolella is the author of four collections of poetry: *Terra Firma* (1990), *Lights & Mysteries* (1995), and *Views from along the Middle Way* (2002), all from Copper Canyon Press. *Almost Human* (2017) was the winner of the Dorset Prize from Tupelo Press. His honors include the Lannan Literary Award, the American Book Award, the California Book Award, the Northern California Book Award, and publication in the National Poetry Series. He has taught literature and creative writing for many years in the San Francisco Bay Area.

Ken Chawkin is a publicist, producer and poet. He holds masters degrees in Education and Maharishi Vedic Science, has been a teacher of Transcendental Meditation, worked in sales, and was the Director of Media Relations at Maharishi University of Management. His first poem won Sparrowgrass Poetry Forum's Distinguished Poet Award, which inspired him to continue writing poetry. They published two of his poems. Years later, a collection of haiku was published in *The Dryland Fish,* An Anthology of Contemporary Iowa Poets, followed by poems in *This Enduring Gift, A Flowering of Fairfield Poetry.* Ken maintains a blog called The Uncarved Blog https:// theuncarvedblog.com. He has two grown children.

Patricia Clark is Poet-in- Residence and Professor in the Department of Writing at Grand Valley State University. Author of five volumes of poetry, Patricia's latest book is *The Canopy*. Recent poems appear in *Prairie Schooner, Michigan Quarterly Review, Superstition Review, Salamander,* and *The Feminist Wire*. She has also published two chapbooks of poetry: *Wreath for the Red Admiral* and *Given the Trees*. She was poet laureate of Grand Rapids from 2005-2007. A new chapbook, *Deadlifts*, will appear from New Michigan Press later in 2017.

Lynn Cohen was a student and mentee of Pulitzer Prize Winners Stephen Dunn and W. D. Snodgrass. She is the author of two books, *Dreams and Dreamers* (Blue Light Press, 2010) and *Lonestar Days* (Camel Press 2003), and has had poetry published in many anthologies. Her new book of poems, *Between the Years*, is forthcoming from Blue Light Press in 2017. Lynn teaches at Suffolk Community College. She has lectured on modern and post-modern literature in the United States, France and Ireland and has given poetry readings in the United States and in Ireland.

Flavia Cosma is an award winning Canadian poet, author and translator of Romanian origin, with over 40 books of poetry, narrative and children's literature. Her work appears in numerous anthologies in various languages, and her book 47 Poems received the ALTA Richard Wilburn Poetry in Translation Prize. Cosma's poetry book *Leaves of a Diary* was studied at the University of Toronto E. J. Pratt Canadian Literature during the school year 2007-2008. Cosma's poetry book *Thus Spoke the Sea* was studied at the Towson University (Prof. Alan Britt) during the school year 2013-2014. Flavia Cosma is the director of the International Writers' and Artists' Residency, Val-David, Quebec, Canada, the Director of the Biannual International Festivals at Val-David, and the International Editor for Cervená Barva Press, Somerville, Massachusetts. http://www.flaviacosma.com.

Rachel Landrum Crumble received her MFA from Vermont College. Her work has appeared in *Southern Poetry Review, Louisville Review,* among others, and recently in *Saint Katherine Review, Stickman Review, Sanskrit* and *Rio Grande Review,* and *Reed Magazine*, as well as two anthologies. She has been awarded scholarships to Bread Loaf, Vermont Studio Center, and participated in Vermont College's Postgraduate workshops. She has taught kindergarten through college, and is currently an inclusion teacher at Ridgeland H.S. in Rossville, GA and lives in Chattanooga, TN with her husband and youngest son.

Lori Desrosiers' poetry books are *The Philosopher's Daughter* (Salmon Poetry, 2013), a chapbook, *Inner Sky* (Glass Lyre Press 2015) and *Sometimes I Hear the Clock Speak* (Salmon Poetry, 2016). Her work has been nominated for a Pushcart Prize. She edits *Naugatuck River Review,* a journal of narrative poetry. She teaches Literature and Composition at Westfield State University and Holyoke Community College, and Poetry in the Interdisciplinary Studies program for the Lesley University M.F.A. graduate program.

JP DiBlasi lives and writes in the Hudson River town of Ossining, New York. She is a social worker who provided assessment and referral services at the family reception center established by New York City immediately after 911. At her workplace, children created a patchwork quilt to help them with trauma and grief. She is currently an independent grant consultant for organizations seeking funding for children's mental health programs. A new writer, her poems have been published in *Chronogram, Little Lantern Press* and *Poetry Breakfast*. Her friends love her sense of humor.

Rita Dove is a former U.S. Poet Laureate (1993-1995) and recipient of the 1987 Pulitzer Prize in poetry for *Thomas and Beulah*. The author of numerous books, among them the 2009 tour de force *Sonata Mulattica,* a poetic treatise on the life of 19th century violinist George Bridgetower, and, most recently, *Collected Poems 1974-2004,* she also edited *The Penguin Anthology of Twentieth-Century American Poetry* (2011). Her drama *The Darker Face of the Earth* premiered in 1996 at the Oregon Shakespeare Festival and was produced at the Kennedy Center in Washington, D.C., as well as the Royal National Theatre in London, among other venues. In 1998 the Boston Symphony debuted her song cycle "Seven for Luck," with music by John Williams, under the composer's baton. Among Rita Dove's many honors are the 2011 National Medal of Arts from President Obama, the 1996 National Humanities Medal from President Clinton and 25 honorary doctorates. She is Commonwealth Professor of English at the University of Virginia.

Boris Dralyuk is a literary translator and the Executive Editor of the Los Angeles Review of Books. He holds a PhD in Slavic Languages and Literatures from UCLA. His work has appeared in the *Times Literary Supplement, The New Yorker, London Review of Books, The Guardian,* and other publications. His translations from Russian include Isaac Babel's *Red Cavalry* (Pushkin Press, 2015) and *Odessa Stories* (Pushkin Press, 2016). He is the editor of *1917: Stories and Poems from the Russian Revolution* (Pushkin Press, 2016), and co-editor, with Robert Chandler and Irina Mashinski, of *The Penguin Book of Russian Poetry* (Penguin Classics, 2015). His website is bdralyuk. wordpress.com

Stewart Florsheim has been widely published in books, magazines, and anthologies. He was the editor of *Ghosts of the Holocaust,* an anthology of poetry by children of Holocaust survivors (Wayne State University Press, 1989). His chapbook, *The Girl Eating Oysters*, was published by 2River in 2004. He won the 2005 Blue Light Book Award for *The Short Fall From Grace* (Blue Light Press, 2006). His collection, *A Split*

Second of Light, (Blue Light Press, 2011) received an Honorable Mention in the San Francisco Book Festival.

Diane Frank is author of seven books of poems, including *Canon for Bears and Ponderosa Pines, Entering the Word Temple,* and *The Winter Life of Shooting Stars.* Her friends describe her as a harem of seven women in one very small body. She lives in San Francisco, where she dances, plays cello, and creates her life as an art form. Diane teaches at San Francisco State University, Dominican University, and leads workshops for young writers as a Poet in the School. *Blackberries in the Dream House,* her first novel, won the Chelson Award for Fiction and was nominated for the Pulitzer Prize. She is also editor of the *River of Earth and Sky: Poems for the Twenty-First Century* (Blue Light Press, 2015).

Giulio Gasperini was born in Massa Marittima (Tuscany), Italy, in 1984. He has published poetry, some of it dedicated to the issue of migration, and is a social worker with migrants.

Ross Gay is the author of three books: *Against Which; Bringing the Shovel Down;* and *Catalog of Unabashed Gratitude,* winner of the 2015 National Book Critics Circle Award and the 2016 Kingsley Tufts Poetry Award. Catalog of Unabashed Gratitude was also a finalist for the 2015 National Book Award in Poetry and nominated for an NAACP Image Award. Ross is the co-author, with Aimee Nezhukumatathil, of the chapbook *Lace and Pyrite: Letters from Two Gardens,* in addition to being co-author, with Richard Wehrenberg, Jr., of the chapbook, *River.* He is a founding editor, with Karissa Chen and Patrick Rosal, of the online sports magazine *Some Call it Ballin',* in addition to being an editor with the chapbook presses Q Avenue and Ledge Mule Press. Ross is a founding board member of the Bloomington Community Orchard, a non-profit, free-fruit-for-all food justice and joy project. He has received fellowships from Cave Canem, the Bread Loaf Writer's Conference, and the Guggenheim Foundation. Ross teaches at Indiana University.

Jennifer Givhan is a Mexican-American poet from the Southwestern desert. She is the author of *Landscape with Headless Mama* (2015 Pleiades Editors' Prize). Her honors include an NEA Fellowship, a PEN/Rosenthal Emerging Voices Fellowship, The Frost Place Latin@ Scholarship, The 2015 Lascaux Review Poetry Prize, The Pinch Poetry Prize, and her work has appeared or is forthcoming in *Best of the Net 2015, Best New Poets 2013, AGNI, Crazyhorse, Blackbird,* and *The Kenyon Review.* She is Poetry Editor at *Tinderbox Poetry Journal* and teaches at The Poetry Barn.

Ruth Goring's poetry collections are *Soap Is Political* (Glass Lyre, 2015) and *Yellow Doors* (WordFarm, 2003); she has also published a children's picture book in both Spanish and English, *Adriana's Angels / Los ángeles de Adriana* (Sparkhouse, 2017). Ruth's poems have appeared in *RHINO, New Madrid, Crab Orchard Review, Iron Horse Literary Review, CALYX, Pilgrimage,* and the anthology *Misrepresented People: Poetic*

Responses to Trump's America (NYQ Books, 2017). She edits books at the University of Chicago Press and teaches an editing course at the Graham School for Continuing Liberal and Professional Studies.

Bill Graeser, a Long Island native, has worked as dairy farmer, carpenter, teacher of Transcendental Meditation and is currently the Locksmith at Maharishi University of Management, Fairfield, Iowa. Winner of Iowa Poetry Association's 2012 Norman Thomas Memorial Award, published in *North American Review, Michigan Avenue Review, Lyrical Iowa,* and *Chiron Review.* Author of *Fire in a Nutshell* available at Lulu Press or billgraeser.com

Hedy Habra has authored two poetry collections, *Under Brushstrokes* (Press 53 2015), finalist for the USA Book Award and the International Poetry Book Award, and *Tea in Heliopolis* (Press 53 2013), winner of the USA Book Award and finalist for the International Poetry Book Award. Her story collection, *Flying Carpets* (Interlink 2013), won the Arab American National Book Award's Honorable Mention and was finalist for the Eric Hoffer Award. Her book of literary criticism, *Mundos alternos y artísticos en Vargas Llosa* was published by Iberoamericana in 2012. A six-time nominee for the Pushcart Prize and Best of the Net, her work appears in *Cimarron Review, The Bitter Oleander, Blue Fifth Review, Cider Press Review, Drunken Boat, Gargoyle, Nimrod, Poet Lore, World Literature Today* and *Verse Daily.* Her website is hedyhabra.com

Joy Harjo is a member of the Mvskoke Nation. Her most recent collection of poetry is *Conflict Resolution for Holy Beings.* She has written a memoir, *Crazy Brave,* children's books and is at work on a new album of music and a play that will restore southeastern natives to the origin story of blues and jazz.

Jane Hirshfield's eight collections of poetry include *The Beauty* (Knopf, 2015, long listed for the National Book Award), *Come, Thief,* (Knopf, 2011), *After* (shortlisted for England's T.S. Eliot Prize and named a "best book of 2006" by the *Washington Post, the San Francisco Chronicle,* and the *London Financial Times*), and *Given Sugar, Given Salt* (finalist for the 2001 National Book Critics Circle Award). She is also the author of two collections of essays, *Nine Gates: Entering the Mind of Poetry* (HarperCollins,1997) and *Ten Windows: How Great Poems Transform the World* (Knopf, 2015), and has edited and co-translated four books containing the work of poets from the past. Hirshfield's other honors include The Poetry Center Book Award; fellowships from the Guggenheim and Rockefeller foundations, the National Endowment for the Arts, and the Academy of American Poets, and the Donald Hall-Jane Kenyon Prize in American Poetry. Her work appears in *The New Yorker, The Atlantic, The New York Times, The Times Literary Supplement, Poetry,* and eight editions of *The Best American Poetry.* She is a current Chancellor of the Academy of American Poets.

Lois P. Jones is a recipient of the 2016 Bristol Poetry Prize and was shortlisted for the 2017 Bridport prize. She has work published in *Narrative, American Poetry Journal, Tupelo Quarterly, The Warwick Review* and others. She Poetry Editor of *Kyoto Journal*

& host of KPFK's *Poets Café*. Her debut collection, *Night Ladder*, is a 2017 release from Glass Lyre Press.

Joan Naviyuk Kane has authored several books, most recently *Milk Black Carbon*, for which she has received a Whiting Award, the Donald Hall Prize and the American Book Award. She raises her sons in Alaska and teaches in the low-res MFA program at the Institute of American Indian Arts.

William Kemmett was raised in Boston, Massachusetts. His poems have appeared in numerous poetry magazines and journals, including *Yankee Magazine, Cimarron Review, Defined Providence, Poetry Australia, Poetry East, Gargoyle, Mother India, Seattle Review, Calliope, The Café Review, Iowa Source, The Contemporary Review* and *Hanging Loose*. He is the recipient of awards from the Massachusetts Artists Foundation and the New England Poetry Club and has won two Yankee Magazine poetry prizes. He studied poetry at Harvard University and holds an MFA in writing from Vermont College of Norwich University. The author of two full length books from Igneus Press—*Flesh of a New Moon* (1991) and *Hole in the Heart* (2001)—he is also the author of *Black Oil* (2009, Dead "C" Press) in addition to several chapbooks published by Igneus Press and Wampeter Press. He currently teaches English and writing at Indian River State College and lives with his wife in Port St. Lucie, Florida.

Helga Kidder is a native of Germany's Black Forest region and lives in the Tennessee hills with her husband and dog. She has an MFA in Creative Writing from Vermont College. She is co-founder of the Chattanooga Writers Guild and leads their poetry group. Her poetry has been published in *Comstock Review, Louisville Review, Southern Indiana Review, Southern Poetry Anthology: Tennessee (2014)* and *River of Earth and Sky: Poems for the Twenty-First Century* (Blue Light Press, 2015). She is author of three books: *Wild Plums* (Finishing Line Press, 2012), *Luckier than the Stars* (Blue Light Press, 2013), and *Blackberry Winter* (Blue Light Press, 2016).

Amy King's latest book, *The Missing Museum*, is a winner of the 2015 Tarpaulin Sky Book Prize. Of *I Want to Make You Safe* (Litmus Press), John Ashbery describes Amy King's poems as bringing "abstractions to brilliant, jagged life, emerging into rather than out of the busyness of living." *Safe* was one of Boston Globe's Best Poetry Books of 2011. King is a Full Professor of English and Creative Writing at SUNY Nassau Community College and, as a founding member, serves on the Executive Board of VIDA: Women in Literary Arts. King joins the ranks of Ann Patchett, Eleanor Roosevelt, Rachel Carson and Pearl Buck as the recipient of the 2015 Winner of the WNBA Award (Women's National Book Association). She was also honored by The Feminist Press as one of the "40 Under 40: The Future of Feminism" awardees, and she received the 2012 SUNY Chancellor's Award for Excellence in Scholarship and

Creative Activities. She is co-editor of the anthologies *Bettering American Poetry 2015* and, with Heidi Lynn Staples, *Big Energy Poets: Ecopoetry Thinks Climate Change.*

Daniel J. Langton lives and teaches in San Francisco. His *Querencia* won the Devin's Award and the London Prize. His seventh collection, *During Our Walks*, was published in 2012 by Blue Light Press, and his new collection, *Personal Effects: New and Selected Poems*, was published in 2014 by Blue Light Press. In his early 20's, he lived in Paris.

Rustin Larson's poetry has appeared in *The New Yorker, The Iowa Review, North American Review, Poetry East,* and *The American Entomologist Poet's Guide to the Orders of Insects.* He is the author of *The Wine-Dark House* (Blue Light Press, 2009), *Crazy Star* (selected for the Loess Hills Book's Poetry Series in 2005), *Bum Cantos, Winter Jazz, & The Collected Discography of Morning*, winner of the 2013 Blue Light Book Award (Blue Light Press, San Francisco), *The Philosopher Savant* (Glass Lyre Press, 2015) and Pavement, winner of the 2016 Blue Light Poetry Prize.

Susan Lewis (www.susanlewis.net) is the author of *Zoom*, winner of the Washington Prize (The Word Works, 2018) as well as nine other books and chapbooks, including *Heisenberg's Salon* (BlazeVOX [books], 2017), *This Visit* (BlazeVOX [books], 2016), *How to be Another* (Červená Barva Press, 2015), and *State of the Union* (Spuyten Duyvil Press, 2014). Her poetry has been published in a great number of anthologies and journals, including *The Awl, Berkeley Poetry Review, Boston Review, Cimarron, The Journal, The New Orleans Review, Raritan, Seneca Review, Verse, Verse Daily,* and *VOLT.* She lives in New York City and edits *Posit*, an online journal of literature and art (www.positjournal.com).

Lyn Lifshin is a prolific poet with 130 books and chapbooks credited to her name, including three from Black Sparrow Press: *Cold Comfort, Before It's Light,* and *Another Woman Who Looks Like Me.* She has been published by other numerous presses, such as NYQ Books, NightBallet Press, Texas Review Press, Rubber Boots Press, Kind of a Hurricane Press, Tangerine Press, and Transcendent Zero Press. Lifshin has two prize winning books about short lived beautiful race horses, called *The Licorice Daughter: My Year With Ruffian* and *Barbaro: Beyond Brokenness.* Her recent books include *Ballroom, Katrina, In Mirrors, Persephone,* and *Lost In The Fog.* Other books include *Knife Edge & Absinthe: The Tango Poems, Light At the End: The Jesus Poems,* as well as *All the Poets Who Have Touched Me, Living and Dead: All True, Especially The Lies.* An update to her Gale Research Autobiography, called *On the Outside, Lips, Blues, Blue Lace,* is now out. Also available is the documentary film about her, *Lyn Lifshin: Not Made Of Glass.* Forthcoming books are *The Silk Road* and *The Refugess.* Lifshin can be found at her website, www.lynlifshin.com.

Stephen Linsteadt is a painter, poet, and a writer. He is the author of the poetry collection *The Beauty of Curved Space* (Glass Lyre Press 2016), and the non-fiction books *The Heart of the Hero* and *Scalar Heart Connection,* which are concerned with humanity's connection, or lack thereof, with Nature, the Sacred Feminine, and the global community. Stephen was a finalist in the 2016 Edna St. Vincent Millay Poetry Prize. His poetry has appeared in *California Quarterly, The Tishman Review, Silver Birch Press, Synesthesia Literary Journal, Pirene's Fountain, San Diego Poetry Annual, Gyroscope Review, Saint Julian Press, Poetry Box, Spirit First,* and others. He has published articles about heart centered consciousness in *Whole Life Times, Awaken, Truth Theory, Elephant Journal,* and others. Stephen's paintings were featured in the poetry anthology *Woman in Metaphor* and have also appeared in *The Tishman Review, Reed Magazine, Lime Hawk, Badlands Literary Journal, Birmingham Arts Journal,* and on the covers of various poetry collections.

Ellaraine Lockie is a widely published and awarded poet, nonfiction book author and essayist. Her thirteenth chapbook, *Tripping with the Top Down,* was recently released from FootHills Publishing. Earlier collections have won the Encircle Publications Chapbook Contest, the Poetry Forum Press Chapbook Contest Prize, San Gabriel Valley Poetry Festival Chapbook Contest, the Aurorean Chapbook Choice Award and Best Individual Collection Award from *Purple Patch* magazine in England. Ellaraine teaches poetry workshops and serves as Poetry Editor for the lifestyles magazine, *Lilipoh.*

Irina Mashinski was born in Moscow; she graduated summa cum laude from the Physical Geography Department of Moscow University where she later completed her Ph.D. studies, specializing in Paleoclimatology and General Theory of Landscape. She is the author of nine books of poetry and translations. Her first English-language collection, *The Naked World,* is forthcoming from Spuyten Duyvil. She is co-editor, with Robert Chandler and Boris Dralyuk, of *The Penguin Book of Russian Poetry* (2015), and co-founder (with the late Oleg Woolf) and editor-in-chief of the StoSvet literary project, which includes the *Cardinal Points Journal,* coedited in collaboration with Boris Dralyuk and Robert Chandler and currently published under the auspices of the Slavic Studies Department of Brown University (in English), and Storony Sveta journal (in Russian). She is the recipient of several Russian literary awards, and, with Boris Dralyuk, of the First Prize in the 2012 Joseph Brodsky/Stephen Spender Translation Prize competition.

Nancy Lee Melmon loves the taste of words!! She lives with her husband, Ronny and their Westie, Maxwell, in the Red Rock country of Sedona, Arizona. Nancy believes that writing poetry, arranging and rearranging words on the page is an act of True Power! She has performed the spoken word, her own poems, at the Sedona Arts Center. Nancy also plays classical piano, especially Bach. She has been practicing Qi Gong for many years too, and quite enjoys working with people, using her skills in Eden Energy Medicine, EFT, and the Emotion Code and the Body Code.

Megan Merchant lives in the tall pines of Prescott, AZ. She is the author of two full-length poetry collections: *Gravel Ghosts* (Glass Lyre Press, 2016), *The Dark's*

Humming (2015 Lyrebird Award Winner, Glass Lyre Press, 2017), four chapbooks, and a forthcoming children's book with Philomel Books. She was awarded the 2016-2017 COG Literary Award, judged by Juan Felipe Herrera, the Poet Laureate of the United States. You can find her work at <u>meganmerchant.wix.com/poet.</u>

Gloria Mindock is the founding editor of Červená Barva Press and one of the USA editors for *Levure Litteraire* (France). She is the author of *Whiteness of Bone* (Glass Lyre Press, 2016), *La Portile Raiului* (Ars Longa Press, Romania) translated into the Romanian by Flavia Cosma, *Nothing Divine Here* (U Soku Stampa, Montenegro), and *Blood Soaked Dresses* (Ibbetson St. Press). Widely published in the USA and abroad, her poetry has been translated and published into the Romanian, Croation, Serbian, Montenegrin, Spanish, Estonian, and French. Gloria recently was published in *Gargoyle, Constellations: A Journal of Poetry and Fiction, Muddy River Poetry Review, Unlikely Stories* and *Nixes Mate Review.* She is currently the Poet Laureate in Somerville, MA.

Dorothy Shubow Nelson's book *The Dream of the Sea, Early Poems* came out in 2008. Her poems have appeared in *Polis IV,* 2014; *Human Architecture VII,* 2009: *The Human Promise of Poetry in Memories of Mahmoud Darwish; Consequence Vol. I; Atelier; Café Review; Sojourner;* and other publications. Her review of Bruce Weigl's book, *The Abundance of Nothing,* appeared in *Consequence Vol. V.* Formerly Senior Lecturer in English at UMass/Boston, she facilitates a Veterans Writing Workshop in Gloucester Mass. and serves on the Advisory Board of the Gloucester Writers Center.

Aimee Nezhukumatathil is the author of four books of poetry, most recently, *Oceanic* (Copper Canyon, 2018). With Ross Gay, she co-authored the chapbook, *Lace & Pyrite: Letters from Two Gardens.* Her collection of nature essays is forthcoming from Milkweed. Honors include a Pushcart Prize and a fellowship from the National Endowment for the Arts. She is poetry editor of *Orion* magazine and professor of English in The University of Mississippi's MFA program.

Giuseppe Nibali was born in Catania, Sicily, in 1991, and attended school in Bologna, Italy. He has won several poetry prizes in Italy.

Lin Ostler has authentically engaged with poetry since she established a literary magazine, *Satori,* her first year in college. Teaching literature & writing in Edmonton, Alberta, at Vermont College in Burlington, she has also guided writers' workshops & classes in Utah — all the while being a Yoga Instructor for 45 years, & a single mother. Her first published poem was in the anthologized book, *The Poetry of Yoga.* Lin's embodied, earthy work has been danced & incorporated into multi-cultural collaborations such as *Moving the Stone* and *Emergents—Tracks in the Motherline.*

Her manuscript, *Masquerading as Fire* tied for first place in the Utah Arts Original Writing competition.

Gregory Pardlo's collection *Digest* (Four Way Books) won the 2015 Pulitzer Prize for Poetry. His other honors include fellowships from the National Endowment for the Arts and the New York Foundation for the Arts; his first collection *Totem* was selected by Brenda Hillman for the APR/Honickman Prize in 2007. He is also the author of *Air Traffic,* a memoir in essays forthcoming from Knopf.

David M. Parsons, 2011 Texas State Poet Laureate, is the recipient of an NEH Dante Fellowship to the SUNY Geneseo, the French-American Legation Poetry Prize, and the Baskerville Publisher's Prize. His first collection of poems, *Editing Sky,* was the winner of the 1999 Texas Review Poetry Prize and a 2000 Violet Crown Book Awards Special Citation. His following books, are *Color of Mourning, Feathering Deep, Reaching For Longer Water* (Texas Review Press/Texas A&M University Press Consortium), *David M. Parsons New & Selected Poems* (TCU Press), and *Far Out: Poems of the 60's* (Wings Press, Co-edited w/Wendy Barker). He was inducted into The Texas Institute of Letters in 2009. www.daveparsonspoetry.com

Nynke Passi was born and raised in the Netherlands. She is director of the undergraduate creative writing program at M.U.M. and director of the Luminous Writer literary center. Her work has been published in various literary magazines and anthologies, including *The Gulf Coast Review, The Anthology of New England Writers, Red River Review,* and *River of Earth and Sky.* One of her poems is forthcoming in *CALYX.* Together with Rustin Larson and Christine Schrum, she edited the poetry collection *Leaves by Night, Flowers by Day.* Her story "The Kiss" was nominated for a Pushcart Prize, and her essay "Oom Ealse and the Swan" was a finalist in *The Missouri Review's* Jeffrey E. Smith Editor's Prize '14.

Pina Piccolo, raised in Italy and Berkeley, California, presently living in Italy, has a Ph.D. from the University of California, Berkeley. A poet, teacher, and translator, she is one of the principal coordinators and originators of *La macchina sognante,* an online journal, http://www.lamacchinasognante.com. That journal's focus, and Piccolo's, is on works in translation, frequently treating issues of immigration, racism, history, and non-European cultural realities, as well as encouraging new literary voices.

Robert Pinsky was born and raised in Long Branch, New Jersey. His previous books of poetry include *Gulf Music* (2008), *Jersey Rain* (2000), *The Want Bone* (1990) and *The Figured Wheel: New and Collected Poems 1966-1996.* Among his awards and honors are the William Carlos Williams Prize, the PEN/Voelcker Award, and the

Korean Manhae Prize. He recently received a Lifetime Achievement Award from the PEN American Center.

Connie Post served as Poet Laureate of Livermore, California (2005 to 2009). She runs a popular reading series in the San Francisco Bay Area. Her work has appeared dozens of journals, including *Calyx, The Big Muddy, Blue Fifth Review, Comstock Review, Cold Mountain Review, Chiron Review, Dogwood, I-70 Review, Slipstream, River Styx, Prick of the Spindle, Riversedge, Spillway, Spoon River Poetry Review, Pedestal Magazine, The Toronto Quarterly, Valparaiso Poetry Review* and *Verse Daily*. Her Chapbook *And When the Sun Drops* won the Aurorean's Editor's chapbook award. Her first full length book *Floodwater* (Glass Lyre Press 2014) won the Lyrebird Award. Her awards include the Caesura Poetry Award and the 2016 Crab Creek Poetry Award. This year she was the winner of the 2017 Prick of the Spindle Open Poetry Competition.

Saba Syed Razvi is the author of *In the Crocodile Gardens* (Agape Editions), *Of the Divining and the Dead* (Finishing Line Press), *Beside the Muezzin's Call & Beyond the Harem's Veil* (Finishing Line Press), and the forthcoming *heliophobia*. Her poems have appeared in journals such as *The Offending Adam, Diner, TheTHE Poetry Blog's Infoxicated Corner, The Homestead Review, NonBinary Review, 10x3 plus, 13th Warrior Review, The Arbor Vitae Review,* and *Arsenic Lobster,* among others, as well as in anthologies such as *Voices of Resistance: Muslim Women on War Faith and Sexuality, The Loudest Voice Anthology, The Liddell Book of Poetry, Political Punch: Contemporary Poems on the Politics of Identity.* Her poems have been nominated for an Elgin Award, the Best of the Net Award, the Rhysling Award, and have won a 2015 Independent Best American Poetry Award. She is currently an Assistant Professor of English and Creative Writing at the University of Houston in Victoria, TX, where in addition to working on scholarly research on interfaces between Science and contemporary Poetry, she is studying Sufi Poetry in translation, and writing new poems and fiction.

Suzanne Rhodenbaugh is the author of two poetry books: *Lick of Sense* (Helicon Nine Editions, 2001, winner of the Marianne Moore Poetry Prize) and *The Whole Shebang* (WordTech, 2010); four chapbooks, including *The Shine on Loss,* winner of the Painted Bride Quarterly Chapbook Series; and *The Deepest South I've Gotten and Other Essays* (2017). The essay book includes "Souls in a Concrete Country," written after a 2013 trip to Russia to attend a conference on "Literature and Power." She edited a 19th century diary, published as *Sarah's Civil War* (Bluebird, 2012). Her poems, essays, articles and reviews have been widely published in periodicals. She was born in Florida and raised there and in Georgia and has lived elsewhere in the South, and in the Northeast, the Midwest, and Israel. Since 1999 she and her husband Tom have lived in St. Louis.

George Jisho Robertson is 83 years old, living in Peckham, London, UK in subsidised housing for the elderly and aged, some house-bound. In 1999 he began developing the gardens in Peckham as a wildlife refuge gathering native and rare exotic plants from around the globe. It is an oasis of colour, form and song in a busy multi-cultural district – all the senses are awakened, engaged and at peace. He is a poet, photographer and was a teacher, a senior high principal and later a Zen priest. His poems and essays have been published in *Kyoto Journal, Pirene's Fountain* and *St. Julian's Press* and other publications.

Susan Rogers considers poetry a vehicle for light and a tool for positive energy. She is a lawyer, artist and a practitioner of Sukyo Mahikari—a spiritual practice promoting positive thoughts, words and action. www.sukyomahikari.org Her poetry was recorded for the Pacific Asia Museum's award winning audio tour and is included in numerous anthologies and journals including *Silk and Spice, The Best Poems of San Diego, Kyoto Journal, Pirene's Fountain, Tiferet* and *Saint Julian's Press*. Her poem "The Origin is One" was made into a short film by Yoshikazu Ysa, https://www.youtube.com/watch?v=rzPA9zeC0Qc and was performed at the televised Akigami Ice Festival in Gifu, Japan . She was nominated for a Pushcart in 2013. Lois P. Jones interviewed her for KPFK's *Poet's Café*. You can listen to her poetry at: http://www.timothy-green.org/blog/susan-rogers/

William Pitt Root gratefully acknowledges how much of his own work results from decades spent helping others discover the joys of recognizing and sharing an intensified vision of their own lives and the lives of others by writing and reading poetry. Whether as poet-in-residence among MFA programs of numerous universities and colleges across the country or, via Poets-in-the-schools, working with young people K-12 on reservations throughout the West or with black students still in the theoretically segregated classrooms of Mississippi or with the children of Vietnamese Boat People enclaves in Galveston, what I am shown is the healing power of recognizing, claiming and sharing the truths essential to one's life— and how often it is the "little truths" that carry one through trials and traumas once proclaimed unspeakable. The most recent of Root's dozen collections is *Strange Angels*. His work has been awarded generous grants from Guggenheim, NEA, and Rockefeller foundations.

Mary Kay Rummel was the first Poet Laureate of Ventura County, CA. Blue Light Press has just published her eighth book of poetry, *Cypher Garden*. Her previous collection. *The Lifeline Trembles*, was winner of the 2014 Blue Light Press Award. *This Body She's Entered*, her first book, won the Minnesota Voices Award for poetry and was published by New Rivers Press. *Love in the End* was published as a finalist for the Bright Hill Press Award. Mary Kay's work appears in numerous regional and national literary journals and anthologies, and she has been a featured reader in many venues in the US, England and Ireland including the Ojai and San Luis Obisbo poetry festivals. A professor emerita from the University of Minnesota, she teaches part time at California State University, Channel Islands dividing her time between Ventura, California and Minneapolis.

For the last twelve years, **Becky Dennison Sakellariou** has been living half of each year in Peterborough, New Hampshire, near where her parents lived for over 40 years, and half the year in Greece, where Becky herself lived most of her adult life. Her poetry is infused with the images, words, rhythms and people of both the Mediterranean and New England. She has six books of poetry out, one of which, *The Possibility of Red,* is a bi-lingual edition in both Greek and English, and another, a meditation on breast cancer published by Passager Books, *Gathering the Soft.* Her latest book, a collection of poems from the last five years, *No Foothold in this Geography,* is just out by Blue Light Press of San Francisco. Much of the poetry Becky is writing now centers around the refugee situation in Europe, specifically Turkey and Greece and her experiences in the camps and with the immigrants themselves.

Robert Schultz, the author of five books, has received a National Endowment for the Arts Literature Award in Fiction, Cornell University's Corson Bishop Poetry Prize, and, from *The Virginia Quarterly Review,* the Emily Clark Balch Prize for Poetry. His books include three collections of poetry (*Vein Along the Fault, Winter in Eden, Ancestral Altars*), a novel (*The Madhouse Nudes*), and a work of nonfiction (*We Were Pirates: a Torpedoman's Pacific War*). A native Iowan, he attended Luther College and received his graduate education at Cornell University. In 1985 he returned to Luther, where he taught for 19 years. He has also taught at Cornell and at the University of Virginia. Since 2004 he has been the John P. Fishwick Professor of English at Roanoke College in Salem, Virginia.

Kalpna Singh-Chitnis is an Indian-American poet, translator, actor and filmmaker based in the United States. She received a masters degree in Political Science from Magadh University, Bodhgaya and studied Film Directing at the New York Film Academy in Hollywood. She has also participated in the Silk Routes project of the International Writing Program at the University of Iowa from 2014 to 2016. A former lecturer of International Relations, Kalpna Singh-Chitnis has authored four collections of poems in English and Hindi. Her latest poetry collection, *Bare Soul* was awarded the 2017 "Naji Naaman Literary Award" in Lebanon. She has also received the prestigious "Bihar Rajbhasha Award" given by the government of Bihar, India, for her first poetry collection, *Chand Ka Paivand* (Patch of Moon) in 1987, "Bihar Shri" (Jewel of Bihar) title in 1988 and "Rajiv Gandhi Global Excellence Award" in 2014 for her contributions to literature and cinema. In 2015, she was nominated for the "Honor of Yeast Litteraire" by *Levure Litterarie* magazine in Paris, France, where she also served on the editorial board. Kalpna's poems have been translated into many languages, and her work has appeared in notable journals like *World Literature Today, California Quarterly, Levure Litterarie, The Enchanting Verses* and others. She is the Editor-in-Chief of *Life and Legends* and works on independent film projects in Hollywood. More about Kalpna at – www.kalpnasinghchitnis.com.

Betsy Snider is a retired attorney who lives on a lake in rural New Hampshire with the ghosts of her many cats and dogs. She is a winner of the 2015 Blue Light Book Award for her book of poems, *Hope is a Muscle* (Blue Light Press, 2015). She was first published in *Lesbian Nuns: Breaking Silence* (Naiad Press, 1985). Her poetry has been published in a variety of journals and anthologies, most recently in *The Lesbian Body* (Sinister Wisdom, Fall 2017); *Amore: Love Poems* (Imagination Press, 2016); *Our Last Walk* (University Professors Press, 2016); *River of Earth and Sky* (Blue Light Press, 2015), *Poet Showcase* (Hobblebush Press, 2015) and *Love Over 60* (Mayapple Press, 2010).

S. Stephanie's poetry, fiction, and book reviews have appeared in many literary magazines such as, *Birmingham Poetry Review, Café Review, Cease, Cows, Literary Laundry, OVS, Rattle, St. Petersburg Review, Solidus, Southern Indiana Review, The Southern Review, The Sun* and *Third Coast.* Her three chapbooks are *Throat* (Igneus Press) , *What the News Seemed to Say* (Pudding House - re-released by Igneus Press in 2015), and *So This Is What It Has Come To* (2015 Finishing Line Press) She holds an MFA from Vermont College of Fine Arts and teaches at the NH Institute of Art in Manchester, NH.

Donald Stang has been studying and reading Italian for a number of years. He lives in Oakland, California.

Denis Stokes lives in Callander, Northern Ontario. He was born in Toronto and is a graduate of U. of T. and Vermont College. He has lived in Northern Ontario, Northern B.C. and Northern Quebec. Much of his work has been with First Nations students. He now teaches at Nipissing University. Involved in several sports, the outdoors, the Conspiracy of 3 Reading Series, meditation in the Benedictine tradition and the organization, Development and Peace. He has work in such journals as *Canadian Literature, Quarry* and *CV2.* Works include *Scarborough Poems, Dublin in the Sunlight, A Wolf Rages Down the Little Jocko, Tunnel Jumping* and *The Blackstock Children.*

Paul Stokstad was in the undergraduate poetry workshop at the University of Iowa in 1970-72. His first volume of poems, entitled *Butterfly Tattoo* was published by Blue Light Press in 2012, and has been included in several anthologies, most recently in *River of Earth and Sky* (2015) by Blue Light Press. He taught graduate level Poetry Writing, Advertising Copywriting, Web Marketing and Advertising at Maharishi University of Management for many years, and more recently has served the school in marketing, alumni and fundraising positions. He is an active blogger (pauldejour. com) and has also published books on Tennis, Improv Theatre, Chronic Fatigue, the 2016 Election, and Iowa (see stokstad.com)

Tim Suermondt is the author of three full-length collections of poems: *Trying To Help The Elephant Man Dance* (The Backwaters Press, 2007), *Just Beautiful* (New

York Quarterly Books, 2010) and *Election Night And The Five Satins* (Glass Lyre Press, 2016.)—Pinyon Publishing will publish his fourth full-length collection *The World Doesn't Know You* later in 2017 and MadHat Press will publish his fifth full-length collection *Josephine Baker Swimming Pool*. He has poems published in *Poetry, The Georgia Review, Ploughshares, Prairie Schooner, Blackbird, Bellevue Literary Review, North Dakota Quarterly, december magazine, Plume Poetry Journal, Poetry East* and *Stand Magazine* (England), among others. He is a book reviewer for Červená Barva Press and a poetry reviewer for *Bellevue Literary Review*. He lives in Cambridge (MA) with his wife, the poet Pui Ying Wong.

Arseny Alexandrovich Tarkovsky was born in the Ukrainian city of Elisavetgrad (now Kirovohrad) in 1907 and moved to Moscow in 1923, working as a newspaper journalist and publishing his first poems. By the late 1930s, he had become a noted translator of Turkmen, Georgian, Armenian, Arabic, and other Asian poets. During the Second World War, he served as a war correspondent for the Soviet Army publication *Battle Alarm* from 1942 to 1944, receiving the Order of the Red Star for valor. Tarkovsky's first volume of his own poems, *Before the Snow*, emerged in 1962, when the poet was 55, and rapidly sold out. His fame widened when his son, the internationally-acclaimed filmmaker Andrei Tarkovsky, included some of his father's poems in his films. He died in 1989, just before the Soviet Union fell.

Lynne Thompson won the Tuscon Festival of Books Literary Prize (Poetry) in 2017, the Stephen Dunn Poetry Prize in 2016, and a Master Artist Felloswhip from the City of Los Angeles in 2015. She is the author of *Start with A Small Guitar* (What Books Press, 2015) and *Beg No Pardon* (Perugia Press, 2007) which won the Great Lakes Colleges Association's New Writers Award. Her work has most recently appeared or is forthcoming in *Poetry, Prarie Schooner, Crab Creek Review, African American Review,* and *Salamander* as well as the anthologies *Nasty Women Poets, An Unapologetic Anthology of Subversive Verse* and *Wide Awake, Poets of Los Angeles & Beyond,* among others. Thompson is Reviews & Essays Editor for the literary journal, *Spillway,* and was recently elected Chair of the Board of Trustees at her alma mater, Scripps College.

Jon Tribble was born in Little Rock, Arkansas. He grew up in Aldersgate Camp, a church camp devoted to medical and social services programming just outside of Little Rock. He has worked as a dishwasher, maintenance worker, fry cook, movie theater manager, data processing clerk, and nightwatchman, and he has lived in Arkansas, South Texas, Indiana, and Illinois. He was the recipient of the 2001 Campbell Corner Poetry Prize and he received a 2003 Illinois Arts Council Fellowship in Poetry. He has published poems in print journals, including *Ploughshares, Poetry, Crazyhorse, Brilliant Corners,* and the *Southeast Review*; online, including in *Prime Number, A Poetry Congeries at Connotation Press: An Online Artifact,* and *storySouth;* and in several anthologies, including *The Jazz Poetry Anthology* and *Where We Live: Illinois Poets.* He lives in Carbondale, Illinois, with his wife, Allison Joseph, and he directs internships in editing and publishing for the Department of English at Southern Illinois University Carbondale. He is the Managing Editor of the literary journal *Crab Orchard Review* and is the Series Editor of the Crab Orchard Series in Poetry from SIU Press. He is the author of *Natural State* (Glass Lyre Press 2016), *And There Is Many a Good Thing* (Salmon Poetry, 2017), and the forthcoming *God of the Kitchen* (Glass Lyre Press, 2018)

Political activist and wilderness advocate, **Pam Uschuk** has howled out six books of poems, including *Crazy Love*, winner of a 2010 American Book Award and her most recent *Blood Flower*, 2015, Wings Press. Translated into more than a dozen languages, Uschuk's many awards include the New Millenium Poetry Prize, 2010 Best of the Web, the Struga International Poetry Prize (for a theme poem), the Dorothy Daniels Writing Award from the National League of American PEN Women. Uschuk edited the anthology, *Truth To Power: Writers Respond To The Rhetoric Of Hate And Fear*, 2017, and she's finishing on a multi-genre book called *The Book Of Healers Healing; An Odyssey Through Ovarian Cancer*.

Suzanne Araas Vesely earned a PhD in English Literature under two William Blake scholars of note, Mary Lynn Johnson and John E. Grant. She is the first person to earn an academic track certificate at the University of Iowa Center for the Book. She has also participated in the Iowa Writer's Workshop. As Library Director at Maharishi University of Management, she introduced a cultural events series that is currently administered by Rustin Larson, a nationally recognized poet. Dr. Vesely has published over 30 critical articles in both literature and information science, including peer-reviewed journals such as *Iowa Poetry Review, Iowa Journal of Literary Studies, Colby Quarterly, Walt Whitman Quarterly Review,* and *International Reference Services Quarterly.* She has also organized sessions and made presentations at conferences such as the Modern Language Association and the Kansas Library Association. She is currently working on a book on William Blake's visionary experiences and is also writing her own poetry. She has been deeply involved with world peace initiatives, such as the Global Country of World Peace, for over 40 years.

Christine Vovakes lives in northern California. Her poems have appeared in *The Cape Rock, San Pedro River Review, Poetry Breakfast, Aethlon Journal of Sports Literature, California Quarterly, JAMA, Christian Science Monitor, Boston Literary Magazine, Apple Valley Review, Shamrock Haiku Journal* and the *Marin Poetry Center Anthology.* Her articles and photos have been published in *The Washington Post, Christian Science Monitor, Sacramento Bee* and *San Francisco Chronicle.* Christine participates in the Blue Light Press On-Line Poetry Workshop. One of her short stories won a Patricia Painton Scholarship at the Paris Writers Workshop.

Ocean Vuong is the author of *Night Sky with Exit Wounds* (Copper Canyon Press, 2016). A 2014 Ruth Lilly fellow, he has received honors from The Civitella Ranieri Foundation, The Elizabeth George Foundation, The Academy of American Poets,

Narrative magazine, and a Pushcart Prize. His writings have been featured in the *Kenyon Review, The Nation, New Republic, The New Yorker, The New York Times, Poetry,* and *American Poetry Review,* which awarded him the Stanley Kunitz Prize for Younger Poets. Born in Saigon, Vietnam, he lives in New York City.

Loretta Diane Walker, a multiple Pushcart Nominee, and Best of the Net Nominee, won the 2016 Phyllis Wheatley Book Award for poetry, for her collection, *In This House* (Bluelight Press). Loretta was named "Statesman in the Arts" by the Heritage Council of Odessa. Her work has appeared in various literary journals and anthologies including, *River of Earth and Sky, Her Texas,* and *Concho River Review.* She has published four collections of poetry. Her most recent collection is *Desert Light,* Lamar University Press. Her manuscript *Word Ghetto* won the 2011 Bluelight Press Book Award. Naomi Shihab Nye states, "Loretta Diane Walker writes with compassionate wisdom and insight—her poems restore humanity."

Helen Wickes has published 4 volumes of poetry with Sixteen Rivers Press and Glass Lyre Press. She has studied Italian. She lives in Oakland, California.

Martin Willitts Jr is a retired Librarian. He won the 2014 Dylan Thomas International Poetry Contest; Rattle Ekphrastic Challenge, June 2015, Editor's Choice; Rattle Ekphrastic Challenge, Artist's Choice, November 2016. He has over 20 chapbooks including the Turtle Island Quarterly Editor's Choice Award, *The Wire Fence Holding Back the World* (Flowstone Press). He has 11 full-length collections including *How to Be Silent* (FutureCycle Press, 2016) and *Dylan Thomas and the Writing Shed* (FutureCycle Press, 2017).

Kathabela Wilson created and directs Poets on Site, Tanka Poets on Site, and Caltech Red Door Poets. She holds salons and weekly tanka meetings with her husband Rick Wilson at their home, hosts tanka performance festivals in and around Pasadena, California, and welcomes visiting poets. Kathabela performs with Rick's accompaniment on flutes of the world in museums, galleries, libraries, and the local Storrier Stearns Japanese Garden. She has created more than thirty programs and themed anthologies containing international poets' work. She leads the online Facebook group Tanka Poets on Site, for several years giving daily prompts for tanka writing exercises. Tanka Poets on Site was presented on the Queen Mary at the Tanka Society of America's Tanka Sunday in 2013. She currently writes "Mapping the Artist," a weekly interview series with poets and artists, and hosts a weekly "Poetry Corner" for ColoradoBlvd.net, where she presents many tanka poets. Kathabela (her pen name is Kath Abela Wilson) uses her patient, beautiful 94-year-old mother's Maltese maiden name (Abela) as a centerpiece and inspiration. Kathabela and Rick travel the world together to math conferences (the summer of 2014 marked their fifth trip to China and Japan).

Pui Ying Wong was born in Hong Kong. She is the author of two full-length books of poetry: *An Emigrant's Winter* (Glass Lyre Press, 2016) and *Yellow Plum Season* (New York

Quarterly Books, 2010)—along with two chapbooks. She is the recipient of the 2017 Pushcart Prize. Her poems have been published and forthcoming in *Prairie Schooner, Ploughshares, Plume Poetry Journal, Atlanta Review, The New York Times, Valparaiso Poetry Review* among others. She is a book reviewer for Červená Barva Press in Somerville, MA. She lives in Cambridge, MA with her husband, the poet Tim Suermondt.

Paula Anne Yup grew up in the southwest in a family of modest means. Her mother-in-law insists she lives in the past while her husband is equally insistent that she has a shallow memory. She does have flashbacks caused by bad events in a difficult childhood. Also, learning problems have her struggling with her daily life. She is grateful for her college education and loves to read, to draw and to knit. Sometimes she feels bitter about her life circumstances, but she can't deny that life is an adventure full of surprises. *Making a Clean Space in the Sky* is her latest book.

Contributor Index

Glass Lyre Press

exceptional works to replenish the spirit

Glass Lyre Press is an independent literary publisher interested in technically accomplished, stylistically distinct, and original work. Glass Lyre seeks diverse writers that possess a dynamic aesthetic and an ability to emotionally and intellectually engage a wide audience of readers.

Glass Lyre's vision is to connect the world through language and art. We hope to expand the scope of poetry and short fiction for the general reader through exceptionally well-written books, which evoke emotion, provide insight, and resonate with the human spirit.

Poetry Collections
Poetry Chapbooks
Select Short & Flash Fiction
Anthologies

www.GlassLyrePress.com

CPSIA information can be obtained
at www.ICGtesting.com
Printed in the USA
FFOW03n0607191017
41293FF